*European Monographs in Social Psychology*

# Unemployment

Its social psychological effects

*European Monographs in Social Psychology*

Executive Editors:
J. RICHARD EISER, JOSEPH M. JASPARS, KLAUS R. SCHERER
Sponsored by the European Association of Experimental Social Psychology

This series, first published by Academic Press (who will continue to distribute the numbered volumes), appears under the joint imprint of Cambridge University Press and the Maison des Sciences de l'Homme in 1985 as an amalgamation of the Academic Press series and The European Studies in Social Psychology, published by Cambridge and the Maison in collaboration with the Laboratoire Européen de Psychologie Sociale of the Maison.

The original aims of the two series still very much apply today: to provide a forum for the best European research in different fields of social psychology and to foster the interchange of ideas between different developments and different traditions. The Executive Editors also expect that it will have an important role to play as a European forum for international work.

*Other titles in this series:*

*National characteristics* by Dean Peabody

# Unemployment

## Its social psychological effects

Peter Kelvin
*University College London*

and

*Joanna E. Jarrett*
*University College London*

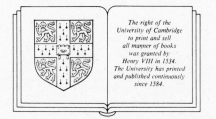

The right of the
University of Cambridge
to print and sell
all manner of books
was granted by
Henry VIII in 1534.
The University has printed
and published continuously
since 1584.

**Cambridge University Press**
*Cambridge*
*London   New York   New Rochelle*
*Melbourne   Sydney*

**Editions de la Maison des Sciences de l'Homme**
*Paris*

Published by the Press Syndicate of the University of Cambridge
The Pitt Building, Trumpington Street, Cambridge CB2 1RP
32 East 57th Street, New York, NY 10022, U.S.A.
10 Stamford Road, Oakleigh, Melbourne 3166, Australia
and Editions de la Maison des Sciences de l'Homme
54 Boulevard Raspail, 75270 Paris Cedex 06

First published 1985

Printed in Great Britain by
Redwood Burn Limited, Trowbridge, Wiltshire

Library of Congress catalogue card number: 84–23276

*British Library Cataloguing in Publication Data*

Kelvin, Peter
Unemployment: its social psychological effects
—(European monographs in social psychology)
1. Unemployment
I. Title   II. Jarrett, Joanna   III. Series
306'.36      HD5707

ISBN 0 521 30481 4   hard covers
ISBN 0 521 31518 2   paperback

ISBN 2 7351 0109 6   hard covers (France only)
ISBN 2 7351 0111 8   paperback (France only)

RB

# Contents

# 1 Introduction*

## Preliminaries

There is nothing new about unemployment – or about social and economic policies designed to cope with its consequences. There are grounds for thinking that the building of the Pyramids, for instance, or the Temple of Jerusalem, were public works, largely undertaken to absorb surplus labour: and certainly the colonisation of Asia Minor in classical times was in part deliberate policy to cope with joblessness in ancient Athens and other city states (Garraty, 1978). In England, and closer to our own time, the systematic involvement of government with the provision for (and control of) the unemployed goes back nearly four hundred years, to the Elizabethan Poor Law of 1601; and that itself consolidated a large array of earlier but much more *ad hoc* regulations. Indeed we shall show that the basic and often contradictory attitudes towards the unemployed in Britain today are the product of a pattern created in the very different conditions of the mid-fourteenth century, and handed down ever since: and we shall argue that much of the quite genuine confusion over what to think, feel, and do about the unemployed stems from the inappropriateness of this pattern. That is for later. The first and salutary fact at the outset is that the unemployed have been recognised and treated as a 'problem' for centuries, but psychological research on the problems of the unemployed themselves spans only the last fifty years.

The beginning can be placed quite precisely in 1933, which saw the publication of both *Marienthal* by Jahoda, Lazarsfeld and Zeisel, and Bakke's *The Unemployed Man*. Since then research on psychological aspects of unemployment has generated a literature of several hundred articles and numerous books (we shall in future refer to this simply as 'the literature'). This material has three broad characteristics: it is descriptive, it is diffuse and fragmentary, and it is almost entirely concerned with the unemployed *man*. It is descriptive in the sense that it has concentrated on painting pictures of the unemployed and of their situation, and only rarely considers underlying processes and implications (important exceptions are Jahoda *et al.*, 1933/72; Eisenberg and Lazars-

* This monograph is in part the product of research funded by S.S.R.C., grant no. HR 6182.

feld, 1938; Komarovski, 1940; Jahoda, 1979). It is diffuse and fragmented in that very valuable information about psychological aspects of unemployment can often be found in sources which are not themselves technically (or intentionally) psychological – not only, for example, in the neighbouring disciplines of sociology and anthropology but also in history and in official statistics. The predominantly male-orientated nature of the research is something which we shall discuss in several contexts. We do stress, however, that it is not due to male 'chauvinism' on the part of the researchers, some of the most distinguished of whom have been women (outstandingly Jahoda and Komarovsky in the thirties; but we shall also refer to valuable contributions in recent years by, for example, Wedderburn, Briar, Hartley, Swinburn). Another basic fact then is that the literature on unemployment deals almost exclusively with the unemployed man, touching on the unemployed woman only occasionally, and in passing.

Within all this we have been particularly concerned with the literature on the *social psychological* effects of unemployment on the relationships of the unemployed individual – with his family and friends, with social service agencies, with potential employers, and, quite broadly, with 'society'. That is all manifestly 'social'. In addition, however, as an integral part of his relationships but less obviously so, we have also been much concerned with the unemployed individual in his own right: with the effects of unemployment on his behaviour in general and on his attitudes – towards himself as well as to others. For the nature of a relationship depends not only on what each participant to it thinks, feels, and does concerning the other: that itself depends on what each thinks and feels about himself; and what he thinks and feels about himself is greatly affected by what he finds himself doing – or not doing. One pattern of response to becoming unemployed, for example, is a sense of not doing anything worth while, and disliking oneself because of this: dislike of oneself makes one uneasy, depressed, or perhaps aggressive: and this sours relationships with others. Equally important, and in some respects often more so, the concept which one has of oneself is profoundly affected by how one is treated by others, or at least by how one thinks one is being treated by them. In other words, an individual's self-concept is in large part *socially* defined – not only by others as such, but also by how he himself perceives his relationships with them. We shall have much to say on the self-concept of the unemployed.

The essence of the social psychological effects of unemployment can be defined in terms of four basic questions:

How does his unemployment affect the way in which the unemployed individual sees himself?

How does his unemployment affect how he perceives others?

How does his unemployment affect the way in which he perceives himself to be seen *by* others?

How do others actually see the unemployed?

and to each of these has to be added the follow-on 'What is this due to, and what effects does it have in its turn?' In the 'real world' some of the most important answers to those questions are, of course, closely connected: how an individual regards himself affects the ways in which he behaves to others, which affects how they treat him, which affects how he sees them ... and so on. These questions do not produce neatly distinct answers. They do however define and clarify the central problems; and in doing so they provide a conceptual framework for examining and integrating information which, without it, would remain even more fragmentary and diffuse.

There is one other, very different, question: 'What is the point of social psychological research on unemployment?' As far as we know the question has not been asked – at least not quite so bluntly; and not by psychologists, who are ultimately the people who have to answer it. There is, of course, the academic case that unemployment is worth study simply as a phenomenon, just as much as, say, the respiration of molluscs or the influence of Norman French on Chaucer. Though one can usually put forward some potential 'use' for such research, in truth it is an intellectual mountain, to be climbed because it is there. The pursuit of the useless is one of the most distinctively human of human characteristics: it is moreover frequently a source of esteem as well as of pleasure – except, significantly, in the case of unemployment. Research can thus be valued and valuable in its own right, even when it is not in any normal sense 'useful'. However, given the undisputed hardship of the great majority of the unemployed, the idea of essentially 'academic' research into their condition may appear almost indecent; and in practice, the motivation and purpose of psychological research on unemployment seems to have been to help the unemployed.

The desire to help is understandable. Unfortunately the fact is that *professionally* there is very little that psychologists as such can actually and directly *do* for the unemployed. There may indeed be a small proportion of the unemployed who seek psychological help, and that proportion might be a little larger if psychological services to the unemployed were expanded. Even expanded psychological facilities, however, would be only a minor adjunct to other services: for the principal agencies for the welfare of the unemployed are first and foremost concerned with their material needs – and in the vast majority of cases very properly so. As we shall argue, there has been a singular failure to distinguish between the psychological effects of unemployment and those of the poverty which usually attends it. It is a failure which has frequently misled not only psychologists but also the medical profession, sociologists (as distinct from social administrators), churchmen, and innumerable others. In the final analysis the psychologist cannot supply either of the two things which most of the unemployed most need: money, or a job which brings money. (A job may also provide for several other important needs, such as a structure to one's activities, membership of a group, a 'place in society', and we shall discuss these later: but psychologists, medical practitioners, sociologists cannot supply the unemployed with those any more than with an income or work.)

Research on the social psychological effects of unemployment is therefore of very little direct use to the unemployed. A case could be made that inasmuch as psychological findings are disseminated they may provide the unemployed with 'insight', and this might help them indirectly, if they can act on its implications. Such findings might also help other people to understand the problems of their unemployed relatives, friends and neighbours, and so smooth relationships with them. All this is true, but these are no more than haphazard palliatives for a profoundly unpalatable situation. It is also not what social psychological research sets out to do, certainly not in most cases.

Fundamentally, social psychological research on the effects of unemployment is concerned with one of several classes of non-economic consequences of this particular economic condition (another important class is the effect of unemployment on health). The function of such research is to identify and explain the non-economic 'costs' of that condition; and these in turn can then be built into the evaluation of policies, not least economic ones. In kind, social psychological research on unemployment belongs to the same category of research as research on the side-effects of drugs or the effects of pollution.

In the case of the side-effects of a drug, for example, or of an industrial process which produces pollution, the drug or the process may offer important, often very important, benefits to the individual or to society. The problem is that these benefits cannot perhaps be obtained without harmful by-products. It therefore becomes a matter of *decision* whether or not the benefits outweigh the harm, or even the mere risk of it: alternatively, we may seek the benefits at less risk, even if at greater costs of various other kinds. Examples abound, ranging from personal decisions about cigarette smoking, to decisions on the conservation of buildings and the countryside, the control of industrial waste, the monitoring of pesticides and drugs, and the development of new forms of energy. In all instances, the function of research, whatever its discipline, is to provide information and to examine its implications from the standpoint of that discipline. Beyond that, however, the applications of its findings in practice always involve further assumptions and value-judgements which lie outside the domain and the discipline of the research itself.

That is the position of social psychological research on the effects of unemployment. It can be seen particularly clearly in the context of high unemployment. One of the main causes of this, both historically and at present, has been the development of new technologies. New technologies usually bring considerable benefits, but they also bring the demise of the methods which they replace, and so the unemployment of those whose jobs thus disappear. What then happens to these unemployed depends – as with other forms of industrial waste – on whether there is investment in other ways in which they might be productive; or whether, through lack of investment, they become jetsam and are left to drift. Whatever the course or compromise, these ostensibly economic decisions will have been significantly shaped by considerations which are essentially non-economic. On purely economic grounds, for example, it is absurd to spend billions on welfare support for the unemployed – billions which are economically unproductive for society but even so barely provide subsistence for most of the recipients. Yet not to provide for them at all would be almost universally regarded as morally inexcusable: and to make provision conditional – say on communal work – would be politically widely unacceptable and impractical in our kind of society. In effect, any answer to the question 'What should be done about unemployment?', even if the answer is 'nothing', has its roots in beliefs about the nature of man and of society.

It is here that social psychological research can make constructive contributions. Social psychology is concerned with what people believe; it is also concerned with how they act; and it is therefore inevitably concerned with the relationship between beliefs and actions. The ramifications within this are, of course, complex. In particular there is the very important difference between beliefs concerning facts and beliefs which reflect systems of value: in the realm of fact the relation between belief and action is essentially a matter of competence, in the realm of values it is a matter of integrity. Since beliefs about man and society encompass both facts and values, the relationship between belief and action can go awry in a variety of ways. For example, there is a taken-for-granted assumption that whatever other differences there might be between individuals in a democracy they are nevertheless equal as citizens. Unemployed people, on the other hand, frequently feel that they are treated as 'second-class citizens': and when one examines the conditions for obtaining welfare benefit, especially means-related benefits, it is quite incontrovertible that these involve invasions of the privacy of claimants which would be deemed intolerable in relation to 'ordinary' men and women. It may well be that these invasions of privacy are justified in order to insure as best one can that limited resources go to those who truly need them. That is not the issue here. The issue is that in becoming unemployed many a citizen becomes a second-class citizen. In a period of high unemployment, moreover, this is likely to be through no fault on the part of the individual. It is, as it were, one of the costs of technological change. It is, however, also incompatible with any basic assumption that a citizen is a citizen, whatever his or her condition. There is then a choice; either we, as individuals, can admit (and not least to ourselves) that recipients of public welfare cannot be treated as full citizens; or 'society', on our individual behalfs, that is in the form of the state and its laws, has to accept that full citizens have rights which some of them may abuse to defraud it.

Unemployment raises a host of problems of various kinds, and most of them are probably not capable of wholly satisfactory solutions. Some, like the second-class citizenship of so many unemployed, are not so much problems of unemployment as of society's attempts to cope with it: inasmuch as this kind of problem is a product of legislation, and 'society' *wants* to solve it, to that extent at least it can be solved by legislation. Other problems, however, seem to be inherent in the basic conditions of being unemployed. The most important example is the consistent evidence that human beings need a sense of purpose and structure to their lives; that the vast majority derive this purpose and structure very largely from their work; and that to be unemployed is therefore for most people deeply disturbing, distressing, and debilitating. It is, of course, possible that if the unemployed had more money, many of them might find new purposes and new structures through developing leisure and other personal activities. The fact is that the great majority of unemployed do not have access to such external resources: is it then valid, or arrogant self-deceit, or sheer cant, to argue that external resources are scarce and yet expect internal ones to be limitless?

Research can discover, inform and explain: it does not itself produce decisions and action. It cannot make us good; it may help to make us honest.

## Scope

Our commentary covers both less and rather more than the conventional 'review' of a literature on which we originally set out. It covers less because it was only when we had had our first look at the material that we realised that there is not just a single psychological literature on unemployment, as we had thought, but there are two – and all *our* questions were concerned with only one of these. It is also less because, in our initial naivety, we had intended to encompass research from anywhere in the world: in the event, although we have examined work done in the United States, Europe, and Australia, and although we shall make use of some of that, most of what we shall have to say has its basis in the United Kingdom; and to what extent, and in what ways, one may generalise from this, is itself a matter for research.

We covered more than we had planned, because the answers to our ostensibly simple social psychological questions took us inexorably beyond the individual into his (or her) situation: into the general economic setting in which the unemployed individual finds himself, into the services and provisions available to the unemployed, and the implications of these, and into the wider social environment of the unemployed. We also covered very much more than would be encompassed by a review of simply the academic social psychological literature. If we had confined ourselves to the strictly academic, we would have had almost nothing to say; there would have been very little to add to Eisenberg and Lazarsfeld's classic review of 1938. We have ranged quite widely. We have included not only substantive contributions from other disciplines, but also articles from ephemera, such as weekly magazines and, occasionally, daily newspapers; such ephemera may be lightweight in themselves, but on several issues they were our only sources of evidence, and on others they provided highly relevant supportive material.

Our central concern was the *effects* of unemployment. Put slightly differently, but usefully for identifying the nature of the problem, we were concerned with *unemployment as the cause* and the behaviour, feelings, and ideas associated with it as effects. It is at this level that the literature on unemployment as a whole splits into two main classes: for there is also a literature which treats psychological and social psychological factors as the cause, with *unemployment* as the effect. That is the perspective of the considerable body of research on the problems of special groups within society as a whole, and on the special programmes for such groups. These encompass the physically and mentally handicapped; people handicapped by their history, say, as alcoholics or ex-convicts: most of them are, however, concerned with the problems of three, often overlapping, categories – the young unemployed, the unemployed of ethnic minorities, and the hard-core, long-term unemployed. This literature probably warrants exploration in its own right, but we shall touch on it only occasionally and in passing. Our present concern is first and foremost with, for want of a better term, the *ordinary* 'unemployed worker' – that is with the effects of becoming and being unemployed on the kind of person who has 'normally' been in work; who has seen himself, and mostly still sees himself, as 'normally' being in work; and who is seen as someone who would 'normally' be working. Inasmuch as an individual is an ordinary worker in this sense, the fact that he may be young or black is irrelevant, and some of the research to which we shall refer certainly included young people and members of ethnic minorities in just this ordinary way. We have, however, mostly excluded studies which concentrated on groups with special problems *because* they were 'special': for in the great majority of these studies the focus has been on the *causes* of their unemployment, any effects being little more than implied. With one major exception, only very few studies of such special groups have so far explored the interaction between causes and effects – as in the case of sub-cultures which are partly a response to and then partly a cause of difficulties in getting work (e.g. Triandis *et al.*, 1975). The one major exception is research on the relationship between the length of time for which an individual has been unemployed, and the effects of this on himself and on his chances of finding work: that interaction is well documented; it can happen to the most 'ordinary' of employed workers; and it raises problems which we shall indeed discuss in several contexts. We shall not, however, deal with the problems of special groups as such: for inasmuch as the people involved belong to groups which are, and are seen to be, 'special', this may profoundly complicate and confound any analysis of the causes and effects of their unemployment. Or it may not: but until we have some grasp of the general pattern of effects on the ordinary unemployed worker, we do not even have a rational basis for the questions we might ask concerning those with special problems.

The other constraint which we had to impose on ourselves stems from a kind of ignorance which is almost unavoidable. The effects of unemployment do not occur in a vacuum, but within particular environments: not only in particular social but also in particular economic and physical environments. We have a certain amount of knowledge and understanding of the situation in this country, and where we recognised that we did not know something we needed to know we mostly had reasonable access to relevant information: we have no equivalent personal knowledge of the situation in other countries, nor any reasonably practical access to equivalent information concerning them. We will take two examples. First, the way in which an individual responds to being unemployed must be assumed to be significantly affected by the level of *provision* which his society makes for its unemployed, and by the conditions on which that provision is available to them. We know something about this in relation to the United Kingdom; we know almost nothing, or truly nothing, about the situation in other countries. To overcome such ignorance would, in practice, require a multi-national team; in the absence of such a team, international comparisons cannot be more than superficial, except in being misleading. Secondly, different places have different *climates*. Astonishing as it may seem, we have not found a single study which has looked systematically at the effects of climate on reaction to unemployment. Every now and again one encounters passing references to weather, for instance to the additional distress caused by a hard winter (e.g. Zawadski and Lazarsfeld, 1935): but controlled studies and comparisons there are none. Yet it must surely make a difference whether one is unemployed in Newcastle upon Tyne or Newcastle, New South Wales, in Wigan, or San Diego – if only in terms of the clothes one wears, and of being in- or out-of-doors. Among psychologists, however, climate, presumably because it is part of the taken-for-granted personal background of the researcher, has been ignored.

Climate, and the levels and conditions of provision for the unemployed, are hard facts: differences between countries on these counts constitute differences in the most basic physical and material circumstances of the unemployed – even before one considers more general, and generally rather vague, 'cross-cultural' differences. (The French term for unemployment, *chômage*, derives from 'to take one's ease during the heat of the day'; *un jour chômé* is 'a day off' (Garraty, 1978, p. 4). The literature has, for all practical purposes, nothing to say on these matters: whereof one cannot speak, thereof one must be silent.

At least perhaps one should be. In fact, of course, one cannot write sensibly about the effects of unemployment without reference to fundamental and 'classic' work such as Komarovsky's *The Unemployed Man and his Family* (1940), from America, and especially the study of *Marienthal*, from Austria, by Jahoda *et al.* (1933/72). We shall also make use of other American research, and a little from the Netherlands, Australia, and Japan. Nevertheless, we are very aware that the literature with which we have been concerned is, with very few exceptions, essentially an English-speaking literature. We have nothing from Scandinavia and Germany, and we particularly regret that we have nothing from France, Italy, or Spain – that is, from the more southern and Catholic parts of Europe (Marienthal, in Catholic Austria, had no church: we shall return to this). This is partly because our computer searches listed scarcely any material from these sources, and partly because our own resources in terms of languages are limited. More fundamentally, however, we know that we could not in any case have assessed that literature with any confidence, let alone validity: we simply do not have the necessary grounding in the circumstances of other countries; and without that grounding one cannot sensibly discuss the psychology of their unemployed. We have, in effect, been deliberately parochial in that even within the English-speaking literature we have concerned ourselves primarily with British material on the British situation. It is at this level that we have covered rather more than we had envisaged at the outset.

Our initial questions were essentially cognitive – how did unemployment affect the way in which an individual saw himself, how did it affect the way in which he perceived himself to be seen, and so on. In trying to find the answers, it became increasingly clear that one has to consider the general settings in which the unemployed individual operates, and his experiences within these. Examples of this are the search for work; the factors which shape search strategies, and the consequences of failure to find work; the conditions for obtaining benefit, and particularly the social psychological implications of these conditions; the domestic economy, and the general economic environment of the unemployed; the perspectives of agency staffs (primarily Benefit Office staff) and of employers; the complex and contradictory nature of Public Opinion – and numerous other factors. All this in turn took us beyond the strictly 'social psychological' literature, and also sometimes well outside the strictly 'academic': we had, for example, to foray into 'social adminis-tration', and a little into 'economic history' and economics; and on a number of issues the relevant evidence was, as we have said, in ephemera, and not in books or learned journals. We certainly do not claim to have a full set of 'answers', but, by ranging as we did, we have, we believe, clarified a number of questions; and for some of these we can at least point in the directions where the answers might be found.

We ourselves, then, have of necessity to concentrate mainly on British material. The chances are, however, that much the same *questions* could be asked in other countries: and which of them yield similar answers, and which different – and why – is in fact the only way to discriminate between local patterns of response to unemployment, and to identify any truly general ones.

## Sources

We began, for all practical purposes, as newcomers to the psychology of unemployment. We had read *Marienthal*, and Marsden and Duff's *Workless* (1975), the review of the literature of the Depression by Eisen-berg and Lazarsfeld (1938) and other odd pieces. In retrospect these three provided probably the best and most stimulating introduction to the field. They still do; and for 'basic' reading we would only add to them Bakke's *The Unemployed Man* (1933), and Komarovsky's *The Unemployed Man and his Family* (1940). Although not 'psychological', there is also much to gain from the quantitative research of Daniel's *A National Survey of the Unemployed* (1974a; also Daniel and Stilgoe, 1977; Daniel, 1981); and from the social administrative perspective, of Sinfield's *What Unemploy-ment · Means* (1981). Finally, Garraty's *Unemployment in History* (1978) provides an important but almost invariably neglected historical back-ground.

Aware of how little we knew, we began with a computer search. This covered *psychological abstracts, sociological abstracts, dissertation abstracts, ERIC* (an 'educational' data base), and the *Magazine Index* (subsequently we also made use of the *British Humanities Index*, which was not on computer). The search was defined by the key-words 'unemployed', 'unemployment', and their synonyms, linked with psychological key-words such as 'responses to', 'self-concept', 'self-esteem', 'attitudes to', and so forth.

Our main search yielded 529 articles and books whose titles seemed pertinent. We were able to obtain and scan 416 of these. The remaining 113 were books or articles which were not available in this country; and their authors, where we were able to locate them, did not reply to us. We have used the term 'scan' of the 416, because on looking beyond their titles most of them quickly emerged as irrelevant. It was in fact looking at these which clarified the irrelevance, for our purposes, of almost all material on 'programmes' for the hard-core unemployed: most of these were concerned either with people who had special problems, or with the unique problems of a special and often remote region of the United States – for instance on an Indian Reservation. Much of the work on unemployment from the 1950s to around the early 1970s seems to have been on such special problems (e.g. Hutson and Smith, 1969; Doeringer, 1969): we shall return to this shortly.

The final bibliography consists of over 300 titles of articles and books, 157 of which stem directly from the computer search. The remainder are references which we found in these initial sources, chance encounters, the references to which those pointed in their turn, and so on. We are bound to have missed material: we hope we have covered enough to provide at least a general starting-point for the exploration of more specific issues.

## Definitions, and related problems

One of the most difficult problems of research on unemployment is to define who is to be regarded as 'unemployed'. From a psychological standpoint (as distinct from, say, an economic one), there are three main classes of definition of the unemployed: the bureaucratic definition, functional definitions, and self definitions. Psychologically these definitions all overlap; they are all relevant, but they are also all inadequate, singly and in combination. This is not being academically pedantic or destructively critical: we simply must point out that there is a problem here; it probably cannot be solved satisfactorily, but it is essential to recognise it. At the bureaucratic level, the term 'unemployed', as we now use it, goes back to only the 1880s. Before that, the unemployed were just one element within the largely undifferentiated mass of 'The Poor', provided for, if at all, under Poor Law. By the early 1900s it was becoming increasingly accepted that unemployment was 'a problem of industry' (Beveridge, 1909/31), and that the unemployed constituted a special category with special needs – for example, for Labour Exchanges (akin to our Job Centres), as well as unemployment insurance:

it had become 'a paramount need for us to make scientific provision against the fluctuations and setbacks which are inevitable in world commerce and national industry...' (W. S. Churchill, speech of 10 October 1908, quoted Churchill, 1967, p. 303, see also pp. 312–13)

Out of this grew the National Insurance Act of 1911, which provided cover for a limited number of trades and at levels fairly closely related to contributions: 'it laid no great money burden on the state and should be distinguished clearly from the post-war "dole"' (Ensor, 1936, p. 516). That dole ultimately grew into the general provision, only loosely linked to contributions, of our own times.

The details of this history do not concern us. The crucial point is that once the unemployed have become a special category, specially provided for by the state, the definition of who is 'unemployed' is profoundly affected by the state's criteria of who should be entitled to its provision. The problem is that the essentially administrative and sometimes political criteria of the state are by no means always adequate by the functional criteria of, say, the economist or psychologist. For example, it is well known that there is a large number of married women who are unemployed, but who do not register as such because they would not be entitled to any benefit. These women are therefore not unemployed for bureaucratic purposes: they do not, for instance, feature in unemployment statistics, neither are they a charge to the public purse. From an economic standpoint, however, they are functionally unemployed, inasmuch as they are actively looking for work and are thus part of the work-force: and inasmuch as they see themselves as 'normally' in a job, but unable to obtain one, they are also 'unemployed' from a psychological standpoint, and not least in terms of self-definition. On the other hand, there are people who are entitled to benefit, and claim it, and in doing so are theoretically looking for work; yet it is clear to all concerned that on grounds of health or age – near retirement, for example – they are not seriously in search of employment: they neither see themselves as, nor are they more than marginally, part of the work-force. Then there is that small percentage who claim and get benefit as 'unemployed' but also work at least occasionally 'on the side', in the 'informal economy': to that extent they are functionally part of the effective work-force; they may not see themselves as unemployed in the same sense as those truly without work; but they certainly count among the 'unemployed' for bureaucratic purposes.

The problems of defining who should count as unemployed, and of measuring unemployment, have for long been a source of controversy (for example Beveridge, 1909/31; Bosanquet and Standing, 1972; Boon, 1974; Field, 1977b; Forrester, 1977; Sinfield, 1981). The issue recurs again and again. The inescapable fact is that the administration of provision for the unemployed in an industrial society is a complex undertaking, on a very large scale, which could not possibly proceed without bureaucratic criteria. The criteria cannot be more than approximate, and the definition of the unemployed in terms of them is therefore bound to be inadequate: they may be capable of improvement, but they are always likely to err by including either too many or too few.

In practice, most empirical studies of the unemployed seem to have selected their samples on essentially bureaucratic criteria: most, for instance, appear to be based on people who are registered as unemployed, or whatever the functionally equivalent term for 'registered' might be; or they would qualify for being so registered. Given that defining the unemployed is problematic, that is by no means unreasonable: most unemployed do meet these criteria and, with some exception for unemployed married women, the registered unemployed do in effect constitute the majority of the unemployed. Within this, however, there is a further factor – obvious once stated, important, and yet repeatedly neglected, especially by psychologists: namely the level of unemployment at the time of a given study, both generally in the country in question, and in the particular localities of the fieldwork. We shall consider this issue in detail later, but it is also highly relevant as part of the basic background of existing psychological research on unemployment.

The minimal historical facts about levels of unemployment in the United Kingdom are summarised in table 1. We have taken roughly the last 100 years: to provide a general anchor in the period up to the first of the two great wars; to set out the situation of the twenties and thirties; then of the fifties and sixties, and in more detail the seventies and early eighties. The bases of percentages change: those for up to 1914 are from Beveridge (1909/31); those from 1921 onwards are from *The Department of Employment Gazette*, and its fore-runners.

Two particular details need to be added to the figures in the table. First, the unemployment level in 1920, which we do not show, was 2.4%. The massive jump to 17.0% in 1921 (the real beginning of the period) was *not* due to demobilisation after the 1914–18 war: that had been accomplished relatively smoothly by the autumn of 1919, and the great majority of the men returning from the war had at first been readily

Table 1. Percentage of unemployed, United Kingdom: 1880–1982 (base of percentages vary)

| Years | Mean | S.D. | Low | High |
|---|---|---|---|---|
| 1880–1914 | 5.4 | 2.4 | 2.1 (1889) | 9.6 (1886) |
| 1921–1930 | 12.4 | 2.5 | 9.7 (1927) | 17.0 (1921) |
| 1931–1939 | 15.9 | 4.4 | 10.7 (1937) | 22.0 (1932) |
| 1950–1969 | 1.8 | 0.4 | 1.1 (1955) | 2.5 (1968/9) |
| 1970–1974 | 3.0 | 0.5 | 2.0 (1970) | 3.8 (1972) |
| 1975 | 3.9 | | | |
| 1976 | 5.4 | | | |
| 1977 | 5.7 | | | |
| 1978 | 5.6 | | | |
| 1979 | 5.2 | | | |
| 1980 | 6.8 | | | |
| 1981 | 10.5 | | | |
| 1982 | 12.4 | | | |

absorbed by industry. What had happened was that industry had planned for an expansion of trade, not least in exports, which never materialised; and government substantially increased its take in taxation, while at the same time slashing its own expenditure (Taylor, 1965). Second, demobilisation after the war of 1939–45 was not only staggered over a much longer period, but was also followed by National Service. National Service cannot, however, wholly explain the very low levels of unemployment between 1950 and 1970: the last conscript entered the forces in November 1960. At the earliest, unemployment began to rise only in 1967; it did not begin to rise steadily until 1975, and sharply not until 1980. (For other European countries, see B.R. Mitchell, *European Historical Statistics, 1750–1970*, 1975. In general the patterns are broadly similar, but the sources of data vary very considerably.)

*Levels of unemployment are directly relevant to psychological research on unemployment, and to the assessment of its findings.* General levels of unemployment are primarily a function of general levels of economic activity. Very simply, when there is a lot going on almost everyone can find a job; when there is little, almost anyone can lose the job he has. It follows that those who are unemployed at a time of low unemployment are likely to have special problems, for whatever reasons; while in a period of high unemployment the unemployed will consist in increasing numbers of essentially 'ordinary' people down on their luck. There are partial exceptions to this: even at times of generally low unemployment, some particular industry or locality may be hit by particular difficulties, so that 'ordinary' people become special through their exceptional situations (e.g. Wedderburn, 1964, on English Electric Aviation Ltd; Briar, 1977, on the Seattle recession of 1970–2). The generalisation, however, is valid, and is clearly supported when one looks at the *nature* of the literature on unemployment of different periods. Eisenberg and Lazarsfeld's classic review of the literature was published in 1938. Though they did not limit themselves explicitly to research of the 1930s, that is what they did in fact: only two of the titles listed in their bibliography are dated in the 1920s, and one of those is marginal. By the early 1930s most Western industrial nations had experienced some ten years of *high*, often desperately high, levels of unemployment: it had by then long affected the most ordinary of ordinary people: and Eisenberg and Lazarsfeld's domain of enquiry was the *psychological effects* of unemployment.

From 1950 to 1970 was a period of historically quite unprecedentedly low unemployment. This was so, with local exceptions, throughout Western Europe and the United States, as well as in the United Kingdom. Inasmuch as there is a psychological literature concerning unemployment over this period, it is predominantly a literature on 'programmes' for the 'hard-core' unemployed, for the 'hard-to-employ', for the virtually 'unemployable'. These were not programmes for the economic development of depressed areas: they were programmes for the rehabilitation and training of people with special problems – people who seemed not to want a job, or could not find one, or did not or could not hold on to it when they briefly had one. The aims of the programmes were first and foremost to overcome the lack of motivation, confidence, and skills of such people, and the alienating effects on them of belonging to certain sub-cultures, and of the experience of prejudice. As we noted earlier, the programmes were principally concerned with the psychological *causes* of an individual's unemployment, and with combating these: and the literature consists mainly of evaluations of this or that particular programme (there are exceptions to this, e.g. Goodman and Salipante, 1973; Triandis *et al.*, 1975).

As an empirical generalisation, when unemployment is high, psychological research (and the literature based on it) is primarily concerned with the psychological effects of unemployment on the ordinary person: when unemployment is low, it is primarily concerned with the psychological causes of the unemployment of individuals who have special problems. This is not a 'criticism': research in the real world simply tends to reflect the priorities of that world and its situation at a given time.

Situations and priorities change. We have written of levels of low and of high unemployment. Absolute levels are, however, only one of two basic aspects of unemployment: the other is *rate of change* in levels, and for some aspects of our problem, rate of change is more important, psychologically, than absolute levels. Once unemployment has stabilised at a particular level, people adapt to it: it becomes accepted as the base line. Thereafter, response is not to this 'steady state', nor to minor and gradual departures from it, but to marked and rapid change (cf. Helson, 1964, on adaptation level; and Dabelko, 1976, for an interesting experiment on the influence of government statistics in setting the standard for what become 'acceptable' levels of inflation, poverty, unemployment).

The phenomenon can be clearly seen in relation to unemployment. Concern with the 'unemployed', identified as such, first came politically to the fore (in the United Kingdom) with Joseph Chamberlain in 1885–6, and again with Winston Churchill (and Beveridge, and others) in 1908–9: on both occasions this was a response to sudden sharp increases in unemployment (1883 = 2.6%; 1884 = 7.15%; 1885 = 8.55%; 1906 = 3.6%; 1907 = 5.6%; 1908 =7.8%). That was too early to expect psychological research on unemployment. One might, however, have expected psychological research in the 1920s. In fact, Eisenberg and Lazarsfeld, as we noted, cite only one relevant but modest title for that period; nor did we find anything substantive when we ourselves systematically combed *Psychological Abstracts* for the twenties. Unemployment was certainly high for most of the 1920s, but this high level was also relatively stable – until 1930–1. Then it jumped: in the United Kingdom from 10.5% in 1929 to 16.00% in 1930 to 21.00% in 1931. The Austrian numbers – interesting because of the importance of the study of *Marienthal* – rose from 182,000 in 1928, to 192,000 in 1929 and then to 243,000 and 300,000 in 1930 and 1931 (the tables for Austria provide numbers, but not as a percentage of the work-force: Mitchell, 1975). Other countries experienced very similar sharp increases. In effect, the rate of change between about 1929–30–1 was quite exceptional – and that is where we find the beginning of research, which had yielded around 100 titles by the time of Eisenberg and Lazarsfeld in 1938. Much the same has happened, and is happening in our times. The fifties and sixties were essentially dormant, except for research on 'programmes' for the hard-core unemployed, and for the occasional, localised case study. Marsden and Duff (1975), who may justifiably be regarded as the 'pioneers' of our time, began their fieldwork in 1972. By present levels, and by those of the twenties and thirties, unemployment then stood at the almost idyllic low of 3.8%: but it had jumped from 2.6% to 3.4% between 1970 and 1971, an increase of 48%, and that after twenty years with a stable average of 2%. There were further sharp rises between 1974–5–6 of over 40%, and between 1980–1 of 54%: and with these came further concern, and further research.

It is not only psychologists, economists, and other interested specialists who are aware of and react to aggregate unemployment. Levels of unemployment, and rates of change of these levels, are 'news'. Certainly in the United Kingdom, the monthly publication of unemployment figures is accompanied by official comment on the latest figures, as showing an increase or decrease in the rate at which unemployment continues to rise (as it still does); and that in turn is disseminated through all the main media. Thus, although the ordinary man or woman may not be aware of the precise details, they inevitably develop a 'feel' for the general situation. The employed are affected by this as well as the unemployed, but for the unemployed it is especially important: it shapes their perception of their situation, and of their position within it. It is, for example, the source of the phenomenon of the 'discouraged worker' (Flaim, 1973), which we shall encounter in several contexts. Levels of unemployment, and rates of change in these levels, are fundamental aspects of the problem of unemployment: in the aggregate they determine the kind of persons who are unemployed; at the level of the individual, awareness of them is an integral part of his or her socio-economic environment. Psychologists cannot, as they have done, leave such facts entirely to others; they have to learn to use them systematically themselves.

It will be most interesting to see how society, and the research community within it, will respond when present levels of unemployment stabilize and then eventually turn down. As a species we seem to respond more readily to negative feedback than to positive (for very good reasons). The chances are that re-employment will arouse rather less attention and research than unemployment – even though, as we shall indicate, re-employment, too, has its problems. Meanwhile, we were ourselves drawn into this research only by the sudden change in the rate of unemployment in the later half of the seventies, and its increasingly high actual levels. We belong to our time: our enquiry is into the *effects* of unemployment.

# 2   The stages of unemployment

Those concerned with the psychology of work have long stressed that work provides much more than merely money; those of us who are concerned with the psychology of unemployment must now equally stress that to be unemployed is to be poor. Many of the problems of the unemployed stem directly from their financial hardships, and even those whose origins are in themselves purely social and psychological are made infinitely worse by poverty. Behaviour in response to unemployment is the outcome of complex interactions between the psychological condition of the individual and the economic circumstances of his household. These interactions develop and change over time the longer an individual faces unemployment and experiences its concomitants. For instance, economic factors, in the strict sense, cannot have any effects when an individual first hears that he will lose his job, but there is clear evidence that the mere anticipation of the loss of one's job causes considerable stress, at a physiological as well as psychological level (Cobb, 1974; Kasl, Gore, and Cobb, 1975; see also Wedderburn, 1964; Hershey, 1972). At the other extreme, as we shall see later, when prolonged unemployment has brought real poverty, it is very largely the conditions and consequences of that poverty which determine the behavioural effects of unemployment. The progress from these first to final effects of becoming unemployed has been summarised in 'The stages of unemployment'. The literature on these stages begins in the 1930s; its essentials have remained virtually unchanged ever since and, at a descriptive level, the overview which it provides of the effects of unemployment has indeed all the usual advantages of simple generalisations. It also has disadvantages, particularly if one wants to go beyond the phenomena to the processes which underlie them. For example, although there is widespread recognition that unemployment brings both economic and psychological problems to the people affected by it, consideration of the relationship between these problems is quite remarkably rare. There is, of course, a general awareness amongst psychologists of the poverty of the unemployed, and among economists, social administrators, and the political scientists, there is often a considerable sensitivity to the psychological damage wrought by being out of work. Nevertheless, there seem to have been very few attempts indeed to trace the *interaction* of the economic and psychological effects of unemployment. The one clear-cut exception, and even that one only partly so, is of course the study of *Marienthal*, by Jahoda *et al.* (1933/72). It is still the only study which seems to have examined the link between the level of a household's income and the *quality* of response to unemployment by its members, especially by husband and wife. (The careful and in themselves very valuable quantitative studies by Daniel were not concerned with the quality of life. Daniel, 1974a; Daniel and Stilgoe, 1977.) Using broadly behavioural criteria, which covered practical coping strategies as well as attitudes, the research team categorised the unemployed families of *Marienthal* into four groups: unbroken, resigned, in despair, and apathetic; the monthly income of these four groups declined in almost equal steps – from an average of around 34 Schillings per month among the 'unbroken', to barely over half that amount (19 Schillings) among the 'apathetic'. The connection between the type of overall coping response and level of household income was evident. It was, however, only towards the close of the report that there came this late but important realisation,

We have distinguished four basic attitudes: the predominant one is *resignation*; a more active one we named *unbroken*; and two deteriorated forms we called *in despair* and *apathetic*. As we look back on these two forms, it now appears that they are probably but two different stages *of a process of psychological deterioration that runs parallel to the narrowing of economic resources and the wear and tear on personal belongings.*                    (Jahoda *et al.*, 1933/72, p. 87: final italics ours)

The notion that responses to unemployment constitute a *process* which goes through several *stages*, a notion which was little more than an afterthought in *Marienthal*, has since become a basic concept in accounts of the psychological effects of unemployment. Thus, although they may not have used the term 'stages', numerous observers during the thirties were clearly aware of some form of progressive deterioration in the reactions of the unemployed. Beales and Lambert (1934) collected *Memoirs of the Unemployed*, and found a pattern of change from optimism to pessimism to fatalism. Bakke (1933) gave a relatively detailed account of such deterioration. The study of *Men without Work*, by the Pilgrim Trust (1938), which is often careful and perceptive in detail but conceptually naïve, noted an intermediate 'stage' to pauperism, during which individuals became indifferent to independence and increasingly, and passively, accepted what was provided for them.

Most interesting perhaps, though this may only be our own hindsight, is the development of the concept of 'stages' across three publications which involved Paul Lazarsfeld. A concept of stages is, of course, treacherous: in particular there is the need to define the criteria which distinguish one stage from another, and that in turn leads to problems about the number of stages involved. In *Marienthal* (1933/72) there is mention of only two stages, from despair to apathy, although no reason is given why the other two conditions identified in that study, unbroken and broken, might not also be regarded as stages, earlier in the process: for as we saw, differences in quality of coping response were clearly correlated with level of household income over all four types. At the other extreme, Zawadski and Lazarsfeld (1935) listed six stages, in the form of 'changes of mood': first (1) reactions to the dismissal itself, with a sense of injury, fear, sometimes hatred, fury, desire for revenge; then (2) numbness and apathy, replaced by (3) calming down, some adaptation to circumstances, a trust in God, fate, or one's own ability and a belief that things will soon get better; however (4), this hope fades as one finds that one's own efforts are futile and when (5) the situation worsens, *savings* and *resources run out*, there is hopelessness and fear, of winter, of hopelessness; and after that comes (6) acquiescence or dumb apathy and 'the alternation between hope and hopelessness, activity and passivity, *according to momentary changes in the material situation*' (Zawadski and Lazarsfeld, 1935, p. 235; our italics). These six stages are either too many or too few: the distinction between fading hopes (5) and hopelessness (6) is a matter of nuances which would often be very hard to discriminate; on the other hand there would seem to be a profound difference, psychologically, between trusting in fate, in God, 'or' (their word) in one's own abilities, all of which are listed under (3). This particular formulation is therefore perhaps best regarded as a warning to guard against too many 'stages'.

Which brings us to 1938, when Eisenberg and Lazarsfeld produced their article on 'The psychological effects of unemployment', a review of the literature on the psychology of unemployment, European and American, covering the years 1930 to 1938. They concluded

We find that all writers who have described the course of unemployment seem to agree on the following points: first there is shock, which is followed by an active hunt for a job, during which the individual is still optimistic and unresigned; he still maintains an unbroken attitude.

Second, when all efforts fail, the individual becomes pessimistic, anxious and suffers active distress: this is the most crucial state of all. And third, the individual becomes fatalistic and adapts himself to his new state but with a narrower scope. He now has a broken attitude.    (Eisenberg and Lazarsfeld, 1938, p.378).

Since Eisenberg and Lazarsfeld undoubtedly provided the definitive review of the psychological literature on unemployment of their time, and since that time is the only well-documented precedent for our own, their findings have inevitably much influenced comtemporary ideas, not only among psychologists (e.g. Hayes and Nutman, 1981) but quite generally – through articles in 'serious' weeklies and professional journals such as Hill's in *New Society* (1978) and Harrison's in the *Department of Employment Gazette* (1976). Indeed, although Harrison himself ultimately adopts a four-stage format (reminiscent of Beales and Lambert, 1934) he opens his very concise and lucid general review by quoting the very same passage from Eisenberg and Lazarsfeld which we have just quoted. It is thus this version of the findings of the thirties which has come to be most widely known, and this version has lost a crucial theme which runs throughout the primary sources of the period, including the earlier work of Lazarsfeld himself: there is no mention here of the role of poverty, of the loss of savings, of the real and justified fear of harsh winters, of the visible deterioration of one's condition through the wear and tear on personal belongings which one cannot afford to replace. It is symptomatic of the approaches of our own time that Sinfield (1974) is almost exclusively concerned with poverty, Harrison (1976) comments on both financial hardships and psychological effects but scarcely relates the two, and Hill (1978) provides an up-to-date variant of the three-stage model which is often most perceptive behaviourally and psychologically, but makes no reference at all to poverty. We have, it seems, become too specialised.

Yet although that 1938 review lacks the earthiness which links psychological states with tattered clothes and fears of winter, it raises the issue of such a link, at least by implication, at a level of high abstraction. This is in the few sentences which follow the much cited passage on the 'stages'. The passage continues,

Of course, there are large individual differences but one would suspect that the various types of attitudes maintained are more a function of the stage of unemployment than anything else, though there is no doubt that they are also a function of the other predisposing factors that have been discussed above. It would seem instructive to map the course of events for those beginning unemployment with differing attitudes. *It may be that all have the same course, except that the unbroken take a longer time before becoming broken than those who begin as distressed or broken individuals.* (Eisenberg and Lazarsfeld, 1938, p. 378; our italics)

In effect, Eisenberg and Lazarsfeld suggest that any differences between individuals may affect the *timing, but not the course*, not the ultimate psychological outcome, of unemployment. So, having devoted one-third of their review to the effects of unemployment upon personality, they finally came to regard prolonged unemployment as a potential leveller of individual differences. It follows that there must come a point or period of transition, such that an individual's prior personal characteristics (his 'personality') largely cease to shape his response to unemployment, and instead he is himself shaped by that unemployment, and its attendant poverty. This point was developed in the earlier paper by Zawadski and Lazarsfeld (1935) which attributed the behaviour of the final stage 'to the momentary changes in the material situation of the workless' (p. 235). The differences which distinguish individuals require the means to express them: when one's resources barely reach what one needs for subsistence, there is scant margin for self-expression; and when one cannot drive events according to one's own predisposition, one comes to be driven by these events, much like everybody else who is similarly exposed to them.

The notion that the changes in behaviour during unemployment constitute a sequence of stages has become so basic in contemporary discussions of unemployment that it could easily become a 'paradigm' for research. The danger is that we may become so fascinated by the elegance of a 'stage' model that we mistake the convenient sub-division of a continuous process for an explanation of its products: yet to describe a given individual's behaviour as, for instance, 'typical of the second stage in adjusting to unemployment' is scarcely to offer an explanation. The important task for psychology is not to identify and refine 'stages', but rather to identify the factors which determine *transitions* between them. Thus while there is certainly considerable evidence which supports the division of reactions to unemployment into a sequence of stages, and while this may be of value in a variety of ways, from a psychological standpoint it might be more productive to think in terms of '*critical periods*'. Periods of transition from one major stage to another would clearly be 'critical' in this sense, but so also might be periods within stages. There is, for instance, a little study by Alfano (1973) which suggests that attitudes towards work undergo less change during the first month of unemployment than in subsequent months, and that this period might be the most productive for employment counselling and job placement.

Having suggested that psychologists should move from looking at unemployment in terms of 'stages' to looking instead for 'critical periods' in responses to unemployment, we have to admit that we have scant evidence for the validity or usefulness of our suggestion. The fault, however, lies not in ourselves but in a fundamental and inescapable limitation of almost all the existing research on the course of behavioural change during unemployment. For all practical purposes, there is *no longitudinal* study specifically concerned with or designed to explore substantive *psychological* effects of unemployment. The one truly systematic longitudinal study which we have encountered is that reported by Cobb (1974) and Kasl, Gore and Cobb (1975), deservedly well known but, of course, overridingly concerned with *physiological* change and illness-behaviour, not with the unemployed individual's behaviour in the world at large. We found one other explicitly longitudinal investigation by Ohashi (1975a, b), on job-changes and resocialisation of unemployed Japanese miners: but although there were points of interesting detail which emerged from this work, and which we shall cite in other contexts, its approach was very simple, and certainly could not trace, and did not trace, gradual changes in the behaviour of individuals. The literature which we examined, which encompassed the most prominent material of the thirties and all that we could identify and obtain from around the mid-1950s onwards to 1980, yielded only one account of repeated observations over time. This is a report by Bakke in *The Unemployed Man*, of one individual whom he had met three days after that individual had become unemployed, and whom he had followed up through four meetings over seventeen weeks: and Bakke describes how this man changed from self-confident optimism to sullen despondency, but not yet complete discouragement (Bakke, 1933, pp. 64–7). Bakke also cites a second case over time, but rather more briefly, and beginning only after that second individual had already been out of work for two months. To this must be added that the families of *Marienthal* did keep diaries: however, these diaries were not analysed in detail, or at least not reported in detail; and the researchers openly regretted that it was simply not feasible for them to observe family life over time (Jahoda *et al.*, 1933/72).

If we therefore turn to the mainstream of social psychological research, the evidence for 'stages' in response to unemployment stems from three principal sources. There are studies in which at least some subjects were, or seem to have been, interviewed on more than one occasion (e.g. Jahoda *et al.*, 1933/72; Bakke, 1933; Marsden and Duff, 1975); to these 'psychological' sources may be added Daniel, and Daniel and Stilgoe (1977), whose policy-orientated research provided valuable information to which we shall refer later. Second, but rare, there are planned cross-sectional studies, which systematically sampled in terms of the varying length of unemployment of their subjects (e.g. Hill *et al.*, 1973). However, probably the most influential have been the various collections of autobiographies, memoirs, and case histories, and the unstructured components of structured research, all of which in different ways record what subjects wrote or said about their reactions to unemployment over time (e.g. Jahoda *et al.*, 1933/72; Bakke, 1933; Beales and Lambert, 1934; Zawadski and Lazarsfeld, 1935; the Pilgrim Trust, 1938; Komarovsky, 1940; Wedderburn, 1964; Gould and Kenyon, 1972; Marsden and Duff, 1975; Briar, 1977; Hill, 1978). This autobiographical and case-history evidence has made a deep impression: partly because it is very evocative, and therefore emotionally convincing; and partly because, within this, it does indeed convey the *gradual but cumulative* erosion of life through unemployment: it therefore provides the most substantial body of evidence on its psychological effects over time. But impact on the imagination, however valid in its own right, is not an adequate test of scientific validity: and the scientific validity of any of this research, and of all of it, is no more than that which in other contexts would be regarded as that of a pilot study. The complex six stages of Zawadski and Lazarsfeld, for example, were based on 57 auto-biographies, themselves selected, and *not* by Zawadski and Lazarsfeld themselves, from a collection of 774 biographies. Beales and Lambert (1934) derived their optimism–pessimism–fatalism sequence from 25 'memoirs'. Neither Gould and Kenyon (1972) nor Marsden and Duff (1975) elaborated any general account in terms of 'stages' or the like, but their work, and particularly that of Marsden and Duff has had much influence: yet Gould and Kenyon have only 24 cases; Marsden and Duff were essentially concerned with 18 people. Furthermore, the limitation of this evidence lies not only in the size of samples but also in its very nature: as Marsden and Duff pointed out in relation to their own material, when ordinary people talk of their past experiences they may, in their efforts to understand that past themselves, give it retrospectively much greater coherence and continuity than it had at the time.

The chances are that reactions to unemployment do indeed follow a sequence of discriminably different stages: the evidence, although diffuse and in any given instance always flawed, points to this too con-sistently to be dismissed. In principle, therefore, we need to expand it with fuller and systematically planned cross-sectional and, perhaps especially, longitudinal research. What is questionable is whether this is feasible – and even more whether its outcome would be either intellec-tually significant or practically useful.

Cross-sectional studies are certainly feasible, though they would require very careful exploratory research to define the most productive points in time at which to draw the sample. In particular, from a psycho-logical standpoint the most productive times might not be the safe middle of a stage but, on the contrary, the critical periods of transition between one stage and another – if such transition can be identified for cross-sectional sampling. A priori, the great asset of a longitudinal approach is that it is much the more likely to disclose these critical periods. As between the advantages and drawbacks of, respectively, one-shot and repeated interviewing, in an imperfect world one has to choose. The truly serious practical problem of longitudinal research, research which began at the time of job-loss and continued into adap-tation to long term unemployment, would be the very high rates of wastage. Hill's evidence (1978), for example, suggested that the 'settling down to unemployment' begins after about 9 months to a year. In 1976/

77 however, approximately the time in question, only very few of the total of registered unemployed had been continuously unemployed for a year or longer (cf. *Department of Employment Gazettes* for the period).

Some kinds of people are of course much more vulnerable to long-term unemployment than others. It is this differential vulnerability to unemployment of different groups which makes us question the validity and value of the search for a *general* pattern of reactions to unemployment. An assumption of generality underlies all the various existing stage models, for instance those of Beales and Lambert and of Eisenberg and Lazarsfeld in the thirties, and of Harrison, and of Hill in the seventies. However unwittingly, this literature has thereby created a *general stereotype* of the behaviour of the unemployed, with all the potentially misleading over-simplification which this implies. Yet we know, for instance, that skilled and unskilled workers differ in several important ways in their experience of and reaction to unemployment; and we have known this since at least the 1930s, in fact for quite as long as there have been stage-models (e.g. Bakke, 1933; the Pilgrim Trust, 1938; Goodchilds and Smith, 1963; Marsden and Duff, 1975; Briar, 1977). We have also long known of differences due to age (e.g. Beveridge, 1909/31; the Pilgrim Trust, 1938; Daniel, 1974a; Ohashi, 1975a,b; Daniel and Stilgoe, 1977; Hill, 1978; Berthoud, 1979). Some of the simplest as well as some of the most sophisticated research among the unemployed of our own time has been into differences related to cultural background and racial prejudice (Feldman 1973a, b; Triandis *et al.*, 1975). And cutting across all these are differences in the situation of men and women (Jahoda *et al.*, 1933/72; Pilgrim Trust, 1938; Daniel, 1974a; Sinfield, 1979; 1981). To cite all these is not to be obsessionally in search of subtle nuances: these are no more than the most basic of demographic variables, and they are directly relevant to unemployment, to reactions to it, and to any attempt to understand and aid coping with it. We stressed earlier the need to identify and examine critical periods: as an example, therefore, probably one of the most critical periods for an unemployed skilled or professional worker is that which surrounds the decision of whether to continue in one's previous line of work, with all one's previous investment in it, or to change direction; this issue scarcely, if ever, arises for the unskilled. Whether we look at Bakke's men of the 1930s or Marsden and Duff's of the 1970s, six or eight months of unemployment have very different meanings for the skilled and for the unskilled. To subsume both after, say, four months of unemployment under the same all-embracing concept of a 'second stage' or 'intermediate phase' is neither empirically valid nor conceptually constructive.

We have therefore come to the conclusion that while it might be possible to delineate a general stage-model of responses to unemployment, its generality would be at too stultifying a level of over-simplification. The most consistent evidence is that for a 'final' stage of fatalism and apathy. Even in this, the conditions of our time may allow more variability than was available – or at least put on record – in the thirties. There are hints of a black economy in both Bakke (1933) and in the Pilgrim Trust Report (1938). There is rather more evidence for it in recent years (Marsden and Duff, 1975; Jenkins, 1978; see also Gershuny and Pahl, 1980); and it is certainly not confined to the unemployed. The informal economy may, however, be particularly significant in relation to the unemployed, for the unemployed individual who has access to and partakes in it is psychologically not defeated, not apathetic – whatever else he may be in law.

There is a clear consensus of evidence that in the great majority of cases *prolonged* unemployment eventually leads to resignation and to apathy. The fact that the ultimate position may be the same for all does not entail that they all get there in the same way: the levelling of individual differences in resignation and apathy is significant precisely because the starting-points and intermediate stages will so often have been very different. The description of stages does not itself provide an explanation of the effects of unemployment; at most it is merely the first step towards it, and that only if the description is sufficiently accurate. A general model may simply not be able to achieve the necessary accuracy, because its very generality obscures essential differences – differences due to levels of skill, age, regional traditions and experiences, ethnic background and hostilities, and so forth. Yet major demographic and reference-group variables such as these are intrinsic to the central problem with which we are here concerned: that is, to isolate the factors which determine the stages of reactions to unemployment, and especially those which determine transitions between stages and developments within them. We have found only one instance when this was attempted, namely on the very first occasion when the concept of stages was tentatively put forward in *Marienthal*, when Jahoda, Lazarsfeld and Zeisel suggested and explored a *systematic* relationship between increasing poverty and the stages to defeat. Since then we have only had descriptions.

# 3   Looking for work

Psychologically the most critical period for an unemployed individual is that between the initial stage of confidence that one will find work and a final state of tacit or even avowed resignation to unemployment (Alfano, 1973). There are probably numerous 'stages' within this transformation, but of these we know little. What we do know is that between confidence and resignation is the search for work, and its failure. The factors which determine events during this time, and their outcome, are crucial to the development of the unemployed individual, and therefore to the social psychology of unemployment. Yet, although this period is so crucial, there is no coherent literature on the search for work. All that we can try to do is to give a rough shape to an inchoate collection of numerous little bits of information.

To begin with some basic facts – at least about the United Kingdom. Of a sample of nearly 12,000 people who had lost their last job and had not found another, 86% were looking for work: only 14% had fundamentally decided to withdraw from the labour market: over half of these were near retirement age, the others had withdrawn on grounds of health, and for family or domestic reasons. The sample included women and, from the age distribution, many of the withdrawals for family reasons may be attributed to the raising of children. Of those actively seeking work, 73% felt that it was important that they should find it; among the 25 to 35 age group the proportion was 84%; and among the 35 to 45 age group it was 79%. A very influential factor is the presence and number of children: of those who were married but without children 39% felt it 'very important' to find a job as soon as possible; this becomes 62% of those with one to two children, and 73% of those with three or more children. I cite these facts from Daniel's *National Survey of the Unemployed* (Daniel, 1974a, pp. 28, 29, 31). At the time of writing, this is still the most comprehensive published survey of the unemployed of the United Kingdom. The fieldwork dates to November 1973. If anything, in the strict sense of the word, the probability is that a similar survey undertaken today (1985) would show even higher proportions to whom it was 'very important' to find work: in 1973/74 unemployment in the United Kingdom was 2.7% of the working population; currently it is approximately 12%. It follows that those who *from choice* are 'marginal' members of the work force will have constituted a much larger proportion of the total of unemployed in 1974 than they do in 1981. For the great majority of the unemployed, therefore, seeking work constitutes a genuine and very real problem. Daniel is currently engaged on a longitudinal study of unemployment flow: his interim report of 1981 unfortunately does not cover the search for work.

To get a new job one needs to learn that it exists. This may seem obvious, but it is far from simple. There are several sources of information about work and several methods of obtaining it: these differ in their relevance for different kinds of unemployed people: and the relevance of various sources and methods undergoes important changes, especially as a function of the length of an individual's unemployment. Quantitatively the most substantive work on these issues may be found in Daniel (1974a), Daniel and Stilgoe (1977), Berthoud (1979) and Hawkins (1979). Qualitatively the most illuminating study is still almost certainly the detailed account by Bakke (1933). That study may be 50 years old, and there have of course been important changes in the nature, level, and administration of welfare provision since that time; nevertheless, the tactics and strategies of looking for work which Bakke described, and the factors which underlie them, are very close indeed to those observed more recently by, for example, Wedderburn (1964), Dyer (1973), Sinfield (1974), Marsden and Duff (1975), Briar (1977), Forrester (1977) and Sinfield (1981). And, since they are in many aspects so similar, Bakke's early but very detailed report still has much to offer.

Sources of information about jobs fall into two main categories, formal and informal. *Formal* sources, for example, are advertisements, and public and private job-placement agencies. *Informal* sources are family, friends, and general personal contacts. There is one slightly ambiguous third source, direct approaches by an unemployed individual to potential employers. Daniel (1974a) counts these as 'informal'; we shall argue shortly that in their psychological characteristics they are essentially 'formal'. First, however, it is necessary to distinguish between two main classes of job-seekers: the skilled or otherwise qualified, and the unskilled, unqualified. There is, then, a partial interaction between category of source of information and class of job-seeker: while the informal sources of personal contact are very important among all kinds of job-seekers, and very effective, they are especially important and effective for the unskilled, the unqualified. The reason for this may be inferred from the accounts by Bakke (1933), and much the same pattern can be seen in the more recent case studies of Marsden and Duff (1975). Where an individual has skills or other qualifications, these themselves help to *define* his or her situation and domain of search (Form and Geschwinder, 1962; Showler, 1979). Through having something particular which one can offer, it is possible to identify who may particularly want these qualities:

one can recognise which advertisements apply to oneself; an employment agency can match the demonstrable qualifications of the job-seeker against the formal specification of the job; and, by the same token, the individual himself can locate potential employers who might be worth approaching directly (e.g. Bakke, 1933; Wedderburn, 1964; Swinburn, 1981). Bakke explicitly remarked on the precision and economy with which his skilled men looked for work – compared with the long hours of weary, random trudging of the unskilled. Over forty years later, Marsden and Duff reported their skilled men writing letters to likely firms, while the unskilled may go to factory gates or building-sites, but mainly hope to hear of work by word of mouth, and to be introduced by family and friends.

There are, therefore, two generally very different senses of 'personal' contacts as a means of finding work. There is, first, the direct approach to an employer which is 'personal' only as distinct from being made by an agency or as a response to advertisements. Second, there is the 'contact' in the shape of a third person, a relative or mutual acquaintance, who becomes an intermediary between the job-seeker and employer. To treat both these forms of personal contacts as 'informal' is unwise: it obscures psychologically important differences between them. 'Personal contacts' in the sense of intermediaries, of people who know people, may properly be regarded as informal: they derive, ultimately, from the separate interactions between job-seeker and intermediary on the one hand, and intermediary and employer on the other, which becomes a chain linking them all. To make direct approaches to unknown employers, however, is essentially to act as one's own agency: it is intrinsically formal in manner, and 'informal' only in that it by-passes the institutional formalities of bureaucracy.

In *seeking* work, Daniel's data show that most people pursue several methods, be they 'formal' or 'informal'. In terms of effectiveness for *finding* work, however, the data indicate important differences as a function of skill and qualifications; the direct approach emerges from the literature as widely successful among the semi-skilled and skilled, but as almost the least useful tactic for the unskilled; among the unskilled, singly most successful source of work was personal contact (Daniel, 1974a, pp. 71–2). The sample was small, but the general pattern of results is consistent with that of the literature of case studies: for instance, examples of the importance of personal contacts for the unskilled run throughout the accounts of Marsden and Duff. In another context, Banks and Warr (1980) pointed out that an unskilled youngster whose father is unemployed thereby lacks a most important informal network for finding work himself. Conversely, if a working father can be crucial to the young entrant in the world of work, so a working son or daughter may be to help the older worker retain a place within it. Sinfield (1981) cites instances of men near retirement who would almost certainly not have found jobs without the contacts of their working sons. The pattern transcends culture: Ohashi (1975b) tells of the redundant Japanese miner in his fifties who found work in the factory which employed his 16-year-old daughter and his 20-year-old son.

It is typical of the problems of unemployment that one means of solving them is incompatible with another. In the search for work, the value of informal networks militates against mobility. Networks, whether based on the family or friends, depend on people's roots in a locality: they take time to establish. To move, as some of Marsden and Duff's men sadly discovered, is to lose, or at least to loosen, one's close contacts with such networks (Marsden and Duff, 1975; see also Bakke, 1933). The situation may be particularly complicated for skilled and professional people. The very qualifications which identify them and provide work when they are in demand become a limiting factor when they are not. Paradoxical as it may seem at first, the more qualified an individual, the more specialised he tends to be; and the more specialised he is, the narrower the range of openings available to him, though they may indeed be marvellous when they occur. Qualifications restrict the individual's occupational identity, in his own eyes as well as in the eyes of potential employers (Showler, 1979). One important consequence of this is that the well qualified, and perhaps especially professional people, often have to move much greater distances than the unskilled in order to get such work as there is for them (Stub, 1962; though this article is twenty years old, and American, it is an interesting study of an interesting issue). Inasmuch as geographical mobility may be 'forced' on highly skilled and professional workers, for instance in the course of, or in search of, advancement, they may often be too transient to establish firm informal networks in any one locality. This may not matter when there is plenty of work, and when trade and professional associations, with their journals and conferences, provide their members with specialised networks of their own. The problems arise when an individual's skills are no longer in demand: both qualifications and the networks based on them then lose much of their relevance, and, if the individual has been recently mobile, he will have little by way of purely informal networks as an alternative.

Within this there are several features of particularly psychological interest in the operations of employment agencies run by the British government – the erstwhile *Labour Exchanges* and present *Employment Offices/Job Centres*. A very concise but clear account of the establishment of Labour Exchanges, and of the economic and social consideration which prompted this, is provided by Beveridge (1909/31) – a contemporary who had been much involved in these problems from early in the century. There was quite as much recognition then as now that the least qualified were generally the most vulnerable to unemployment, but that to these must sometimes be added those who are skilled but whose skills have become obsolete through technological change. The intention of the Labour Exchanges was to reduce the irregularity of employment of the casual labourer, and to assist efficient mobility of skilled labour by bringing together the employer looking for workers and local workers looking for employment. To this end

the Exchange should endeavour to find for each vacancy the workman who is industrially best qualified and should pay no attention to priority of registration or need ... to promote an advantageous mobility of labour, and not wasteful wandering. (Beveridge, 1909/31, p. 301)

The essentially economic function of the 'Exchanges' in the labour market became linked with the social welfare function of distributing unemployment benefit, the unemployed 'signing on' for work at one desk, and collecting allowances at another. This was the situation up to 1973, and Daniel's sample all followed that procedure: and the Job Centre ('Exchanges') was the most frequently cited source of *information* about work in his report (Daniel, 1974a, p. 71). Daniel however noted that its use as a source of information was inversely related to occupational status – declining as status rose. In terms of *effectiveness*, the Job Centres were most productive for unskilled workers, accounting for 35% of work found; they were also clearly useful for the skilled, but to a rather lesser extent: 23%. As we pointed out earlier, qualifications give access to a wider range of sources and methods of finding work. This then becomes very evident at the 'top': Berthoud's study, undertaken in 1977, found that *Professional and Executive Recruitment* was the least effective and efficient source for professional or executive appointments; for these specialised people, with a clear occupational identity, the effective sources are advertisements, direct enquiries, specialised agencies – and only very low down come acquaintances in the trade and general agencies (Berthoud, 1979, p. 43). That was for the sample as a whole. Significantly, however, this pattern is very different for the 'older', the over-45s: for these the most effective methods were general agencies: next came, as equally effective, specialist agencies and trade acquaintances; Professional and Executive Recruitment was in fourth place; and only some way behind came direct approaches and advertisements. In effect, the pattern of the 'older' executive or professional unemployed, for all his or her qualifications, has more in common with that of the unskilled than with the mainstream of professionals and of executives in their 'prime'.

There is an important social psychological aspect to this. Government agencies should perhaps be especially relevant and productive in relation to the more 'marginal' members of the work-force – the less qualified, the older, the physically or socially disadvantaged, and so on. Yet the 'image' of Labour Exchanges, as handling predominantly marginal workers on the dole, was thought to be itself a handicap which discouraged employers from making full use of the Exchanges.

From 1973 onwards the two functions – matching workers and jobs at one desk and paying benefits at another – were split into different buildings, often far apart. In this way the employment service hoped to escape the dole-queue image and attract more jobs, by moving progressively into Job Centres on high street sites.                                                        (Layard, 1979, p. 3)

The reasons and motives were sound: to be able to help the unemployed it is necessary to have jobs for which they may apply – which means overcoming the resistance of employers and encouraging them to notify their vacancies to the government agencies. However, by separating the job-matching role of the employment service from the dole queue, this new approach also separated the unemployed from the regular, routine exposure and access to job opportunities. In theory, of course, there is nothing to prevent an unemployed individual from going to a Job Centre whenever he wishes; in practice, the demoralising effects and hopelessness induced by prolonged unemployment increasingly makes such visits seem useless and even painful. In its effects, therefore, the self-service system of Job Centres is of greatest use to the *recently* unemployed, and thereby itself much reduces the opportunities for the long-term unemployed. According to Layard 'in 1976, two thirds of all those who had been out of work for over a year had *never* been submitted for a job' (Layard, 1979, p. 4). To this must be added that the employment service, like so much else, succumbed to that most contemptible of late twentieth-century virtues, 'productivity', judged in terms of numbers, and damn the quality. As Layard points out, the service became reluctant to put forward the more marginal candidates: it had become 'a service which increasingly serves the easy-to-serve' (p. 4). Ironically, there is some evidence that, at the other extreme, the service does make a special effort to find jobs for those who have been through its own rehabilitation centres. These people are the 'hard cases' of long standing, who appear to be reluctant to find work, and most of whom only go to rehabilitation centres in response to pressure (Field, 1974; 1977a; Campling, 1978). It seems that in the early 1970s about half these cases subsequently found work.

How was it done? 'To be quite frank' said one genial manager 'we jump the queue. Otherwise our chaps wouldn't stand a chance in hell.'
                                                        (Cohen, 1972, p. 41)

In essence the service here does not act in its 'formal' capacity, as an agency, but fundamentally as an 'informal' network of personal contacts – and everyone gains his Brownie points for productivity. The same seems to happen in the United States (Solie, 1968).

We certainly do not wish to imply that the hardest and most difficult cases should be left to rot; on the contrary, when we briefly return to these re-habilitation centres later, we shall see that they can perform several constructive functions. We simply wish to make articulate a very basic feature of the deeply paradoxical situation of the unemployed. The more marginal and vulnerable an individual is, the more he is in need of help from the employment service provided by the state. That service, however, is in a very difficult position. It has to attract enquiries from employers: to do so, it must ensure that employers have confidence that the applicants whom it sends are 'sound': yet the length of an individual's unemployment itself diminishes his perceived soundness (Beveridge, 1909/31; Bakke, 1933; Sinfield, 1981). In practice, therefore, a recently unemployed person is much more likely to be offered a job than someone who has been unemployed for many months – and ultimately no one is helped if the longer-term unemployed is put forward unsuccessfully, while the potentially more successful newly unemployed waits until he, too, has joined the hard-to-place, long-term, queue. So marginality becomes increasingly the realisation of a self-fulfilling prophesy. The separation of Benefit Offices from Job Centres separated the job-seeker physically, and so perhaps psychologically, from one of the main sources of work, a source particularly important to the most vulnerable section of the work force (Daniel, 1974a; Daniel and Stilgoe, 1977; Sinfield, 1979; 1981).

To summarise, a montage of our various pieces of information yields a small set of first generalisations. Everyone who has access to personal contacts makes use of them. In terms of practical usefulness, however, personal contacts are particularly important to the unskilled and unqualified, not only as a source of information but also as an introduction and often essential personal recommendation. In contrast, the skilled and qualified have the great advantage that they can and do often introduce and recommend themselves, by virtue of the skills and qualifications of their occupational roles: the skilled and qualified can therefore operate more efficiently, independently, and effectively than the unskilled and unqualified. In a sense, the skilled man has only to be identifiable in terms of his *role*; the unskilled has to be credible as a *person* (Marsden and Duff, 1975; on 'roles' and 'persons' generally see Kelvin, 1970).

These are simple first generalisations, and they provide a quite convenient basic 'model' of resources and methods for finding work. They also commend themselves fairly readily to common sense; and they are probably reasonably valid and useful where unemployment is essentially frictional, and the 'skilled' and 'unskilled' conform to the vague stereotypes which we generally have of them. The situation described by Wedderburn in 1964 comes close to these conditions. When unemployment is prolonged, however, and the product of widespread structural changes in industry, these generalisations become inadequate. Difficult economic conditions raise the odds against those who are vulnerable already, and increase the range of those who become vulnerable (Hill, 1970; Hill *et al.*, 1973; Daniel and Stilgoe, 1977). From a social psychological standpoint, three sources of vulnerability and disadvantage are particularly relevant in the present context; age, length of unemployment, and occupational down-grading; the effects of these three often reinforce each other, and the social psychological problems which attend them.

Evidence of the disadvantage of the older worker pervades the literature from its beginning. Beveridge commented on it in his lectures of 1909. Before that, incidentally, in 1907 one of Bernard Shaw's characters in *Major Barbara* had this complaint

I'm only 46. I'm as good as I ever was. The grey patch come in my hair before I was 30. All it wants is 3 pennorth of hair dye ... and I am to be thrown in the gutter, and my job given to a young man that can do it no better than I.

(Shaw, *Major Barbara*, 1907/44, pp. 72–3)

Beveridge returns to the issue in his 1930 lectures, but most of the 'classics' of the early 1930s were so concerned with the general effects of unemployment that they gave little special care to its special consequences for the older worker. From the late thirties, however, we have the work of the Pilgrim Trust (1938), and that explored the situation of the older unemployed in considerable detail (Paterson and Dayly, 1936; Hodge, 1973; Katz, 1974; Burghes, 1977; Colledge and Bartholomew, 1980). In essence, the Pilgrim Trust study concluded: that the older unemployed worker, in his late fifties or sixties, was normally eminently 'employable'; that if he seemed to have withdrawn himself from the labour market, this was in response to the plain fact that employers did not want him; and that employers need to be positively encouraged to take on the older unemployed. For the record, nowadays, that is in the 1970s and 1980s, an unemployed man begins to be 'old' soon after he reaches the age of *thirty-five* (Van Wetzel, 1973), and belongs firmly among 'older workers' when he is in his forties (cf. Daniel, 1974a; Daniel and Stilgoe, 1977): and so technology, which has lengthened the time for which our lives could be useful, shortens the span for which society finds use for us.

It is important to be clear about the nature of the problem: *the older worker is*, and has generally been, *less vulnerable to losing his job* than the young worker; *but if he loses it,* he has much greater difficulty in finding another. The older worker is therefore much more vulnerable to long periods of unemployment, and to occupational down-grading in his search for work. And little seems to have changed over the years. In 1909 Beveridge wrote

The adverse influence of advancing years is thus seen less when it is a question of retaining old employment than when it is a question of finding new employers.

(Beveridge, 1909/31, p. 121)

Nearly 60 years later Marbach reported to O.E.C.D. (Organisation for Economic Co-operation and Development)

The stability, patience, sense of responsibility and experience of older workers are more important than a slight drop in their output.

In most member countries, however, such favourable judgements apply only to workers who have been with the firm some time. When it is a question of taking on new workers, firms openly discriminate against older workers.

(Marbach, 1968, p. 22)

The problems of the unemployed older worker are not new: they are not peculiar to our age, due to newly dismissive attitudes to the older generation, or to exceptional changes in industry, or to some unique narrowness of outlook. On the contrary, far from there being anything new in the situation of the older unemployed, the sad fact is that it is all so unchanged; and it is not just a British or even just a European phenomenon (Van Wetzel, 1973); the same pattern can be seen in case histories from Japan (Ohashi, 1975a and b).

The most careful quantitative research and analyses of the basic situation of the 'older' worker is, once again, that of Daniel (Daniel, 1974a; Daniel and Stilgoe, 1977; Daniel, 1981). This not only confirms the general disadvantages of the older unemployed, but also points to its relationship to the other two problems, length of unemployment and occupational down-grading. The probability of an individual finding work decreases as the length of his period of unemployment increases. In this, too, the attitudes of employers go back a long time, and may have an element of justification. Nearly 100 years ago:

'We have always found' said a large employer of labour, 'as to the artisan, that if he happens to be out of work for 3 months, he is never the same man again.'

(Report of a Special Committee of the Charity Society, 1886, quoted Beveridge, 1909/31, p. 139)

During the early thirties, Bakke reports that

the works managers interviewed said that they found it necessary to link men who had been away from work for even a short period of time with regulars in order that they might 'get back into their stride'. The more skilled the more this would be true. (Bakke, 1933, p. 50)

And in another context, partly related to counselling, Alfano (1973) found evidence that attitudes to work in general may change perhaps particularly rapidly during the first six months of unemployment.

We noted that employers discriminate against older workers (see also *New Society*, 1977). Older workers will therefore tend to take longer to find work. We also noted that employers are reluctant to take on workers who have been unemployed for several months or more; and that employment agencies have in fact learnt not to put forward the longer-term unemployed. Discrimination against the older unemployed thus itself creates the conditions which subsequently seem to justify rejection on the ground of the combination of age and length of unemployment.

To counter this, the older unemployed, more than any other group, have to 'trade down' – to accept lower wages and status, poorer conditions, and higher costs, such as more travelling. This holds not only for manual workers, skilled or unskilled (Barnes, 1975; Daniel and Stilgoe, 1977; Sinfield, 1981) but also for managerial and professional occupations (Dyer, 1973; Berthoud, 1979; Swinburn, 1981). There is some evidence that managerial, professional and scientific workers may have to move much more radically to find work, literally over much greater distances, than other workers (Stub, 1962; Marsden and Duff, 1975); this may be a major factor leading to the relatively high instance of 'early retirement' among the over-55s in these occupations (Daniel, 1974a; Berthoud, 1979). Some no doubt retire early with genuine pleasure: others have little choice but to accept such early retirement as the best of the poor options available to them. Administratively and semantically these people do not belong to our present enquiry; psychologically, however, the chances are that for most who take 'early retirement', this too is a form of 'trading down'.

The position of the skilled or qualified worker was stated very simply by Beveridge; 'the best carpenter in the world is unemployable as a compositor' (Beveridge: 1909/31, p. 135). He went on to observe that the middle-aged man with a trade is often harder hit by unemployment than the unskilled casual labourer – not least because as a skilled man he will have had little if any experience of being out of work. And there is some indirect confirmation of this in more recent case studies: 'qualified people who had had a short spell of unemployment on an earlier occasion reported being less disturbed subsequently, and seemed indeed to be less so than first-timers' (e.g. Wedderburn, 1964; Marsden and Duff, 1975; Swinburn, 1981). However, if his unemployment continues for some time, and begins to seem indefinite, the middle-aged skilled and qualified individual has to cope with the decision which scarcely arises for the younger, and not at all for the unskilled: having spent most of his working life in the occupational identity which he had established for himself, he has to choose between remaining out of work or abandoning his trade or profession (Goodchilds and Smith, 1963; Dyer, 1973; Harrison, 1976). Furthermore, to abandon a trade or profession is not only to lose an integral part of one's identity and status, but also to become 'unskilled' – and perhaps particularly unskilled in handling the situation of being 'unskilled', and in the tactics for finding unskilled work (Barnes, 1975). Throughout all this, also, runs the insidious undertone of declining resources: just when he needs to feel and look his best, to be mobile, to make openings for himself, he becomes aware of his creeping shabbiness, he has to cut down on newspapers, to give up the car, the telephone. The basic pattern was there even in the 'simpler' world of the thirties (Jahoda *et al.*, 1933/72; Pilgrim Trust, 1938): the same problem in our more 'sophisticated' technological consumer society is nicely illustrated in the American study by Briar (1977). We shall obviously return to these matters when we discuss how the unemployed individual sees himself and his situation. For the present we merely want to make articulate something that is constantly ignored unless it is asserted: the *material* consequences of being unemployed, quite apart from any 'psychological' ones, themselves undermine the capacity to find work, and the more so for the skilled and qualified older worker. Again there are no easy solutions, only ironic twists to good intentions. To alleviate the hardship of a possibly long stretch of unemployment, the redundancy paid to miners whose pits were closed was spread over three years. In order to make sure that they would get their full dues, most of the men stayed virtually inactive for these three years. After that, their chances both of finding and coping with new jobs seemed very slim (Goffee, 1978).

For an older unemployed worker, and particularly for a skilled or qualified worker, or for someone who had long been with the same firm, the search for work and the failure to find it erodes his or her occupational identity. Chronologically, and psychologically, the other extreme is the unemployed school leaver, whose failure to find a job delays entry into and development of an occupational identity. We shall consider the deeper social psychological implications of this later. For school leavers too, however, we must assume that reactions to being unemployed will be much influenced by their experiences in search of work.

We know almost nothing about the school leavers' or young people's search for work. It is symptomatic of the problem that the literature of the thirties is, for once, almost wholly irrelevant. The conditions are too different. School leavers have, of course, also been affected by structural changes in industry generally, and perhaps particularly by changes in the distribution and construction industries which were a source of many jobs for young people (Hughes, 1976; Mack, 1977). More fundamentally, however, since the 1930s the school leaving age in the United Kingdom has risen from 14 to 16 years, and adult, or near adult, wages now start at 18 years rather than 21. In the thirties, and earlier, the young school leaver could find work as cheap labour. Then it was the 21 year old who was vulnerable to losing his job on reaching the adult wage scale, often after completing an apprenticeship and therefore much occupational socialisation: there was much bitterness on that account (Bakke, 1933; Pilgrim Trust, 1938). The raising of the school-leaving age, and the lowering of the age of near-adult wages, has much reduced the span of time over which the unqualified young person offers an economic advantage to compensate for lack of experience and qualifications (Sinfield, 1981; see also Pahl, 1978); and though these particular details are those of the United Kingdom, similar problems have been reported in the United States (Sartin, 1977) and of the industrialised economies generally (Melvyn, 1977). If the situation and problems of the older unemployed seem to have changed so little as to suggest the operation of an age-related 'law' (Daniel and Stilgoe, 1977, p. 17) the changes in the situation of the young should make us hesitate to frame it.

About our own time, as we have said, we know almost nothing. This is perhaps largely because although youth unemployment is qualitatively always a very emotive issue, it has only recently become quantitatively substantial. In 1977, for instance, it could be very cogently argued that youth unemployment had been given disproportionate attention (*New Society*, 1977): by the end of 1981, the prospects of the school leaver in the United Kingdom had deteriorated very sharply, and they have continued to deteriorate since. Nevertheless, concern over youth unemployment has not, so far, produced penetrating research into its nature, and especially its practical aspects – in part because the scale of the problem is recent, and there has not been enough time. There have been a few studies into the psychological *effects* of unemployment for young people, which have been nicely reviewed by Carroll (1979; see also Banks and Jackson, 1982). Occasionally, also, one can get glimpses of young unemployed people among the predominantly older samples of the case studies (e.g. Marsden and Duff, 1975; Hill, 1978). These, unfortunately, deal primarily with people who are already 'discouraged'. In the context of this present discussion, however, we need to know what they were like, and how they had acted, before they became discouraged: how they set out to find work, what happened to their various strategies, and so forth. Not even the otherwise invaluable Daniel can help. His 1974 and

1977 studies grouped together all those under twenty-five. His 1981 (interim) report of 'unemployment flow' indicates that his sample includes a number of sixteen and seventeen year olds – but only those who have already 'voted with their feet' to use the adult employment service, rather than, or as well as, the careers service especially designed for school leavers (Daniel, 1981, table v:7): his tables still group together the far from homogeneous '24 or less'. It might be noted that in all these surveys by Daniel, there is evidence that young people may tend to have relatively frequent but essentially short bouts of unemployment between jobs, rather than prolonged continuous periods out of work. It is also noticeable that proportionately more of the youngest age group than the older ones had left their last job of their own accord. These patterns may have changed, or may be changing, during the current depth of recession. Nevertheless, there is a suggestion in these findings that short periods of unemployment may be an integral and recognised part of the search strategies of some young people, and not only of the least skilled. This kind of young person may accept spells of unemployment as the cost of sampling what the world of jobs has to offer: where this is the case, unemployment may be tough financially, but it is unlikely to be very damaging psychologically. If children are brought up to think in terms of worth while jobs, of 'jobs with a future', such sampling would be a fully rational application of their early learning. So would be their rejection of jobs which might be available in certain industries, when the redundancy records of those industries demonstrate the paucity of their prospects (Bourne, 1979). It is, of course, possible that we have missed a major source of information on the job-search strategies of the young unemployed, but it is not very likely. When our examination of the literature had proved unproductive, we made direct enquiries of government departments and agencies, and also of several voluntary and private organisations. They were all most friendly and anxious to help, but in the end could only pass us on, one to another. We can therefore only conclude that so far there has been no substantive research on the ways in which young people (and especially school leavers) search for work, on the strategies which they adopt and why they adopt them, and how they react to, and what they learn from, their successes and failures.

A brief digression is in order on 'programmes' for the unemployed. These programmes fall into three broad classes: those for rehabilitating the hard-core unemployed; those concerned with youth unemployment; and those (seemingly the smallest class) set up to help the structurally redundant. Some, but by no means all, give training in marketable skills; some teach how to look for work, and skills like writing letters and how to act in interviews (Becker, 1965; Beatty, 1975; Blake *et al.*, 1978; Forrester, 1978a). There is evidence that taking part in a programme may by itself enhance self-esteem (Cohen, 1972; Briar, 1977), and some are indeed openly designed to enhance it (Powell, 1973). In some cases, as we noted earlier, those who run the programmes may also be in a position to place their trainees; and for those who have been unemployed for a long time, participation in a programme can provide potentially valuable *recent* references. In all these ways, taking part in a programme may help an unemployed individual to gain employment. It is rather more doubtful, however, whether participation in a programme may properly be regarded as a strategy for finding work, except in the case of programmes explicitly linked with job possibilities. Without such an explicit link, taking part in a rehabilitation programme is essentially a last resort of fading hopes, not a positive strategic choice – and sometimes, of course, it is scarcely a choice at all but merely a response to official pressures (Campling, 1978). It has also been argued that many programmes, and perhaps especially those for the hard-core unemployed, are designed to change only the attitudes and behaviour of the unemployed individual, without changing anything in his situation: yet there is reason to think that especially the hard-core, long-term unemployed may require some special treatment on entry, or long delayed re-entry, to work. Criticism of programmes has been voiced most strongly in the United States (e.g. Friendlander and Greenberg, 1971; Triandis *et al.*, 1974; Bowser, 1974; Beatty and Beatty, 1975; Murray, 1976; Taylor *et al.*, 1977; Albert, 1978); it is, perhaps worth recalling that Bakke, writing of England in the early 1930s, reported on the steps which foremen took to help the unemployed 'get in their stride'.

The literature on programmes warrants a review in its own right. From a psychological standpoint, our sampling of that literature suggests two potentially difficult problems. First, the programmes are highly pragmatic in their approach, and are almost always concerned with solving particular *local* problems, or the problems of very specific groups: the reports on them are therefore essentially in terms of social administration or economic implications, rather than in terms of psychological factors and psychological consequences. Secondly, the programmes inevitably have 'drop-outs'; these are inevitably difficult to locate and follow up: yet from a *psychological* standpoint it is the drop-outs who may be particularly important to the evaluation and development of programmes.

It was not part of our original plan to explore the literature for what it had to tell about the search for work. We had accepted the general assumption that to be unemployed is, for most people, an unhappy state which they strive to reverse. Nevertheless, research has also shown that ultimately the unemployed individual gives up the attempt to reverse it, gives up the search for work, and becomes the 'discouraged worker', who feels that there is no place for him in the labour market, and withdraws himself from it (Wilcock and Franke, 1963; Flaim, 1973; Schweitzer, 1974; Sinfield, 1974; Harrison, 1976; *D.O.E. Gazette*, 1977; Colledge and Bartholomew, 1980). That, in essence, is the last 'stage' of adjustment to being unemployed, in which 'coping' takes the form of mute acceptance. However, that last stage is itself the product of a psychological transformation: we have to go beyond describing the final stage, and *account for the transformation* which turns an individual who once actively sought to change his condition into one who is passively resigned to it. It is not sufficient to merely resort to general concepts such as locus of control (Rotter, 1966; Lefcourt, 1976) or learnt helplessness (Seligman, 1975), tempting as these may be, and valid at some level. There remains the question of how an individual who began by feeling in control came to feel helpless. A most significant part of the answer must lie in what happens to an unemployed person in his search for work: in the skills and strategies he brings to this and the responses which they evoke; in the changes on which he decides, or which are forced upon him. All these will vary, certainly as a function of age and qualifications and length of unemployment, and sometimes of ethnicity and sex. At present the literature on the search for work is still scanty and piecemeal. It is sufficient to support our earliest contention that the model of psychological stages of unemployment greatly over-simplifies (and therefore obscures) very real psychological differences. There has to be a balance, somewhere, between the uniqueness of a case history and the undiscriminating generality of an all-embracing model. Much of that balance will depend on further research and analysis of what happens to different kinds of unemployed people as they search for work.

# 4 The self-concept

## Some underlying processes and basic concepts

The most profound psychological effects of unemployment are on the way in which the unemployed individual comes to see himself. Though these effects will to some extent differ according to an individual's economic situation, fundamentally they are the product of how he, his family and friends, and his society at large, conceive of unemployment and of 'the unemployed'. Those who have written on unemployment have all concluded, or at least asserted, that being unemployed almost invariably undermines an individual's prior status, and deeply damages his self-esteem and general concept of himself. However, while the general conclusions which emerge from various sources may be very similar, and are almost certainly valid, the articles and books which we have found are not a homogeneous lot, dealing with the same issues in the same way. On the contrary, the literature on unemployment and the self-concept, like that on the search for work, consists of bits and pieces, scattered and essentially incoherent. They are found in autobiographical accounts (e.g. Beales and Lambert, 1934; Gould and Kenyon, 1972); only a little less direct are case studies (e.g. Komarovsky, 1940; Marsden and Duff, 1975; Briar, 1977): but various effects of unemployment on the self-concept are also often evident or implicit in the unforeseen consequences of training programmes for the unemployed (O'Leary, 1972); in cultural comparisons (Ohashi, 1975 a, b; Triandis *et al.*, 1974), and even in essentially physiological studies (Kasl *et al.*, 1975). We shall encounter these and diverse other evidence later in this section. In itself all this material, though quite varied, is essentially descriptive and in some respects unavoidably repetitive. Simply to enumerate these findings, therefore, might be useful, but would not take us very much further: it would leave out two partly related and central issues which one cannot avoid once one has actually considered the literature: first, *why* are the job-related aspects of an individual's identity so important, not only to the individual himself but also to others; and *what* is it about the nature of the self-concept which makes it so vulnerable to unemployment? Even only a brief look at these issues, inevitably somewhat speculative, may give some coherence to otherwise often diffuse and different kinds of accounts and research, and help the reader to make his or her own sense of them; something like this is necessary in order to move from description to understanding.

## The importance of unemployment

In a society whose socio-economic structure is still predominantly defined in terms of its division of labour (e.g., Brown, 1978; also Beveridge, 1909/31), the unemployed are defined by what they are *not*, namely *not* part of, not integrated within that structure. This intrinsically *negative definition* of the unemployed has two important and mutually reinforcing consequences. First, it makes the situation of the unemployed individual highly ambiguous, not only to himself but also to his family and friends, and in society in general. To say what someone is *not* tells little of what he is; and even to say what he was, but is no longer, only shows the limits of his past as a guide to his future. In the last analysis, the unemployed labourer, lorry-driver, or lecturer, is no more than a hypothetical future labourer, lorry-driver, or lecturer, and the hypothesis is falsified with every failure to find the appropriate work: and, as in science proper, the psychologically relevant and interesting question is how many falsifications it requires before the hypothesis is abandoned. The second consequence of the negative definition of the unemployed is the assumption (often quite explicit) that they will indeed find work, and thereby once again an identifiable place within society. In effect, although at the macro-economic level we have long recognised that some unemployment is structural, at the truly micro-economic level of the individual we continue to regard the unemployment of particular men and women as in essence frictional. These two consequences reinforce each other, because the ambiguity of the situation of the unemployed enhances the sense that it is (must be, should be) transitory (frictional), and its perceived transience heightens the sense of its ambiguity.

Unemployment is riddled with ambiguities and ambivalences. The facts are mostly not in dispute, the problem is what to make of them; and they are problematic not only for the unemployed individual himself, but also for those with whom he interacts, and for the rest of us, in whatever ways unemployment impinges on us. As with alcoholism and drunks, we may have compassion with the condition as an idea; but we rarely know how to cope with it, and usually seek to avoid those who suffer from it. Ambiguity and ambivalence which cannot be resolved by examining the facts throw us on other people in search for a prescription. What, for instance should be the level of benefits? Not only meanness but also genuine concern for their long-term well-being makes a problem of the level of provision for the unemployed: there are not only the scrounger-hounders but also those who are truly worried about 'pauperisation' (e.g. Beveridge, 1909/31; Pilgrim Trust, 1938; Antebi, 1970; Daniel, 1974; Jahoda, 1979; Sinfield, 1981 – the last three perhaps by implication more than explicitly). Unemployment gives rise to a host of questions of the 'What should one . . . ?' variety; what should one do, think, feel: and the perceived validity of answers rests substantially, though not exclusively, on the perceived consensus of credible others. Thus the social psychological effects of unemployment do not stem simply from the changes in the patterns of an unemployed individual's life, or in his or her general social status. These concomitants of unemployment are certainly important, but even more so are its sheer ambiguities: for the ambiguities induce a coping strategy which is social psychological at the most fundamental level – the strategy of recourse to others to define the situation. Psychologically, as distinct from economically, and for the employed as well as the unemployed, the problem of unemployment is a problem of 'social reality' (Festinger, 1954).

## The self-concept

There are a host of contexts in which it is both convenient and proper merely to assume that we all know what we mean by 'self', whether as a word, or prefix or suffix; in these instances we treat 'self' as a logically 'primitive' term, which we leave to be defined at other levels of discourse. This is what has happened in the context of unemployment, and it is inadequate. Discussions of human consequences of unemployment are full of references to how it lowers self-esteem, saps self-confidence, undermines self-reliance, induces self-disgust, heightens self-consciousness, and so on – all of which cumulatively implies a profound change in the individual's self-concept. If, therefore, we are fundamentally concerned with *changes* in the self-concept, it is very unwise to take it simply and casually for granted that we are all agreed on what the self-concept is: at the very least, it is a useful discipline, and will save time later, to set out some basic assumptions which usually go unexpressed.

We shall assume that the complexities of human behaviour involve complex central processes, such as have at times been labelled 'maps', 'models', 'internal representations', 'plans', 'schema' or 'schemata'. We prefer 'schema', roughly in the sense in which that term was used by Bartlett (1932; see also Miller *et al.*, 1960; Taylor and Crocker, 1981). This preference is almost, but not quite, arbitrary: the connotation of 'maps', 'models', 'internal representations' is essentially cognitive, as, of course, is the connotations of 'self-concept': the concept of 'schema', in the Bartlettian tradition, allows more readily for the inclusion of a 'body-image' as well as of the 'self-concept' within an overall concept of the 'self'. These issues, however, we need not pursue.

*The functions of the self-concept:* for our purposes we do not have to be concerned with the 'self' as some kind of entity, but rather with the functions which a sense of self has for the individual. On that basis, the psychologically most significant fact is that we are *not* normally aware of ourselves. Everyone may have occasional transient episodes of being conscious of himself; but anyone who is markedly prone to this we single out as 'self-conscious', which we regard as at least mildly abnormal, and which we know can become psychologically crippling in severe cases. In one sense, therefore, perhaps the most basic fact about ourselves is that normally we do *not* see ourselves, but simply take ourselves for granted – just as for example we do not normally 'see' the furniture in our home: we are simply part of it, it is part of us. Conversely, possibly the most basic psychological effect of unemployment is that being unemployed itself induces increased self-consciousness, sometimes to a level which becomes disabling.

Precisely because we are not normally aware of ourselves the circumstances which make us so are telling. The ordinary individual becomes aware of himself mainly in situations which, to him, are extraordinary: in strange places, as on moving to a new neighbourhood; with strange people, on first assuming a new job; at strange times, as on waking up to 'I'm on holiday!' At a more strictly physical level, much the same happens on first playing with a new tennis racquet or golf club, using a new typewriter, driving a new car. In their different ways, whether in relation to the 'self-concept' or to the 'body-image', all these situations and tools begin as 'extensions' of the individual which, if they endure, become an integral part of him. This is not analogy: it is precisely what is meant by 'internalisation', whereby the initially novel, and therefore 'external', is incorporated into the schema (new ideas and ways of acting are quite as 'external' at the outset as, say, a new pair of shoes; and some, of course, may never fit, may never be comfortable). Once whatever it is that will be internalised has been internalised, it normally drops out of consciousness – 'normally', not necessarily, nor irretrievably. Once they are in our schema, we simply cease to examine ideas which by virtue of that fact seems self-evident; behaviour which has become second nature; the tools which we use every day. And so, we have a job and an income; we automatically leave our home in the morning, turn left, then right, and catch the bus to work; and there we use our hands and our minds, our shovels, books, benches, calculators, kitchen sinks, or whatever. Until we lose our job. Or even only until we hear that we shall lose it.

Knowledge of impending redundancy is sufficient to force the individual to make articulate a host of assumptions which until then he had taken for granted and set aside as certainties. It forces him to examine his present position and to consider alternative futures (e.g. Wedderburn, 1964). Significantly, performance while still at work seems not to be affected (Hershey, 1972), on-going patterns of job-related behaviour persist; nevertheless, Kasl's thorough longitudinal study has shown quite clearly that the mere anticipation of redundancy induces anxiety and stress (manifested by physiological changes), even when the immediate, concrete day-to-day situation remains virtually unchanged (Kasl *et al.*, 1974; 1975).

It is clear that the schema cannot be a rigid structure, nor is it necessarily always finely tuned, either for input or output. It cannot be a rigid structure, even as a 'record' of past events, because it is constantly updated by feed-back and new information, some of which entails reappraisal of the 'record' itself. As regards fine tuning, this is perhaps essential for some very specific and precise tasks, as in high level perceptual-motor or intellectual skills: mostly, however, the schema can be assumed to operate within fairly broad tolerances, in terms of latitudes of acceptance and rejection, whose general basis is adaptation level. For a full discussion on these matters we must refer the reader to Sherif and Hovland (1961) and to Helson (1964). This is not, however, just 'interesting' academic theorising. The concept of latitude of acceptance is, for example, certainly relevant to the psychological analysis of the search for work, and suggests a methodology for research on this problem: what, for example is the range (latitude) of different jobs which an individual is prepared to accept; what are the factors which determine that latitude; and, even more important, what are the characteristics of shifts in that range, and what induces them? It might be recalled, for instance, that empirical research has shown a relationship (inverse) between breadth of latitude of acceptance and ego-involvement; this may well be highly relevant in coping with unemployment, and for counselling on changes of career (Sherif and Hovland, 1961; Sherif *et al.*, 1965). Similarly, the assumptions of adaptation-level theory may help to account for, and predict, reactions to unemployment as it hits the individual (e.g. Wedderburn, 1964; Marsden and Duff, 1975; Hill, 1978; Swinburn, 1981), and as it may affect society at large (Kelvin, 1980a).

As we pointed out in the introduction, we are primarily concerned with the effects of being unemployed on people who had normally been in regular employment: the special situation of the never or scarcely employed is bound to be different in some important respects, but we shall only be able to touch on these in passing. For the normally employed person, if the self-concept as schema locates the individual in his environment and shapes his interaction with it, then we may regard the effects of becoming unemployed as fundamentally a kind of psychological dislocation; its consequence is disorientation and relocation of the individual, which induces a modification of his schema and self-concept. That, when it is complete, is the final stage of 'adjustment' to being unemployed.

There remains one further set of underlying processes which is also best considered at the outset: the sources of the self-concept – as it were, the nature of the information which shapes it. In principle the origins of an individual's self-concept could be pursued back into his or her infancy, and marked individual differences in the capacity to cope with unemployment may indeed perhaps be partly due to differences in early experience. It is relevant to recall, however, that Eisenberg and Lazarsfeld, whose review was much concerned with personality factors, concluded that the ultimate response to unemployment was much the same for all (Eisenberg and Lazarsfeld, 1938). We touched on this earlier (see p. 21). In any case, inasmuch as, for example, an individual's breakdown is associated with his unemployment but attributed to predisposing factors in his past, the role of unemployment is that of a precipitating event rather than as a prime cause: divorce, for instance, might have been equally catastrophic. Our concern here has to be with effects which can unequivocally – or at least reasonably unequivocally – be ascribed to unemployment.

Unemployment presents the individual with a problem – and a problem, once he is aware of it, is something whose progress and implications the individual consciously monitors. It provides him with two classes of information about himself: first there is the information which he obtains simply from observing himself as he responds to the situation; second, there is the information about himself which is provided by others. This second class of information, which is very important in shaping the self-concept, has itself to be broken down into several subdivisions: there is all that is explicitly said to an unemployed individual in relation to his unemployment, whether critically or supportively; there are the cues which are implicit in the ways in which he is treated by others; there is the impact of the media, encompassing interviews, speeches, reports, documentaries, drama and so forth: and cutting across all of these, there is the unemployed individual's own perception of others – the ideas, feelings, and behaviour which *he attributes* to them in *his* view of *their* response to unemployment, and to himself as unemployed.

*Self-awareness and self-perception:* the first class of information which an unemployed individual has about himself, that which stems from self-observation, can be productively considered in terms of Bem's self-perception theory, and Wicklund's theory of objective self-awareness: both theories have been subject to systematic experimental research (Bem, 1972; Wicklund, 1975; Duval and Wicklund, 1972; Wicklund and Frey, 1980). We clearly cannot go into details here, though it might be noted that these two approaches operate at slightly different levels of analysis, which may make them seem as if they were 'alternatives'. Be that as it may, they provide a number of assumptions which are directly relevant to understanding what happens to the self-concept of the unemployed. Both approaches take it as axiomatic that the human individual has the capacity to observe himself, as if he were an object or another person. Then,

Conscious attention is viewed as dichotomous, having the property of being directed either toward the self or toward the environment ... objective self-awareness will be minimized to the extent that the necessary activities and distractions of ... existence demand attention.

(Wicklund, 1975, p. 237; p. 236)

Individuals come to 'know' their own attitudes, emotions and other internal states partially from inferring them from observations of their own overt behaviour and/or the circumstances in which this behaviour occurs. Thus to the extent that internal cues are weak, ambiguous or interpretable, the individual is functionally in the same position as an outside observer, an observer who must rely upon those same external cues to infer the individual's inner states ... 'What must my (this man's) attitude be if I am (he is) willing to behave in this fashion in this situation?'                                   (Bem, 1972, p. 2; p. 28)

The initial reaction to the onset of objective self-awareness is postulated to be self-evaluation. If the salient discrepancy is negative, the person will be increasingly cognizant of that discrepancy, owing to self-focussed attention. In terms of operations, the discrepancy will loom larger.            (Wicklund, 1975, p. 238)

As we have said, and shall see, the literature on unemployment is rarely more than descriptive. However, it consistently portrays precisely the kinds of conditions and circumstances which, for most people, heighten the tendency to look at oneself as a (somewhat curious) object. They then find themselves puzzled by, and uncertain and ambivalent about, how they are acting and reacting, and wonder what kind of person it is who would act like that: the discrepancy between that person and how they *had* seen themselves, and *want* to see themselves, would mostly be negative; and that would further enhance, at least for a time, their self-awareness.

*Symbolic interactionism:* the second class of information, that which the unemployed individual perceives as the reaction of others to him, can best be understood in terms of the concepts of symbolic interactionism. Where the work on self-awareness and self-perception has its roots in experimental social psychology, the roots of symbolic interactionism are sociology and philosophy (Mead, 1934; Hewitt, 1976; Manis and Meltzer, 1978). By the criteria of experimental research, the empirical evidence for the concepts of symbolic interactionism are somewhat tenuous; and it has also to be said that the label 'symbolic interactionism' is an off-putting instance of truly gothic jargon, all the more perverse in that the approach itself is exceptionally sensitive to the significance of language. Again we cannot go into detail, but several basic assumptions of symbolic interactionism are directly relevant to our concerns. Here, too, it is assumed that the human individual has the capacity to regard himself as an object or 'other' person. The *mechanism* for this is the capacity of the individual to take on the role of others, not least in terms of how *he* looks to *them* (the capacity to assume the standpoint of others is a product of the ability to use symbols). From this derives one of the central notions of symbolic interactionism, that 'we see ourselves as others see us'. Within this, there are at least two kinds of 'others': particular others, as when the individual sees himself from the standpoint (as he construes it) of, say, his doctor, his son, his employer, a social security administrator; and (again as the individual construes him) there is also the 'generalised other', at once an abstraction from particulars into a stereotype, (the 'they'; the 'them') and a personification, as it were, of 'society'. (This is, in a sense, an account of how we become objectively self-aware, of how we make self-attributions.) The assumption that an individual's self-concept is significantly defined by how he is seen, and especially by how he perceives himself to be seen by others, is central to any analysis of the social psychological effects of unemployment. There is, however, a telling paradox in the symbolic interactionist account of the self, or if not quite a paradox, at least a problem. Though we may see ourselves as others see us, we also often take great care not only to present ourselves as we wish to be seen, but also as we believe we 'really' are; and we may seek to avoid those who do not see us as we see ourselves (Goffman, 1969a). Such efforts at presenting and maintaining one's 'real' self imply that the individual has in some sense a reasonably clear concept of himself – a self-concept which may originally have been much influenced by others, but which has become autonomous, as it were internalised. On this basis, the literature on the effects of unemployment may be seen as a record of conditions and processes which undermine the functional autonomy of one's previously taken-for-granted self-concept: the unemployed individual becomes once again exceptionally dependent on how he is seen, and perceives himself to be seen, by others – on external sources to define himself. Psychologically

as well as economically, unemployment is a condition of forced dependence, which makes the individual deeply vulnerable to others: it is a
condition which, if it had not been forced on the individual, would
'normally' be regarded as regression. An intuitive but profound grasp of
this is repeatedly reflected in autobiographical accounts and case
histories: unemployment is felt as a humiliation, not only in many of its
practical consequences but also in its basic nature. That is not, however,
because of the loss of some mystical dignity of work. The feeling of
humiliation is a concomitant of the sense of being so very dependent on
others, psychologically as well as materially – for it is the condition of
childhood, not of mature men. It deeply undermines the self-concept
established before becoming unemployed.

# 5 The unemployed individual as seen by himself

In examining the effects of unemployment on the way in which an individual sees himself, we shall limit ourselves fairly strictly to material based on the self-observations of the unemployed. For the actual people concerned, of course, the ways in which they see themselves inevitably merge with how they perceive themselves to be seen by others: nevertheless it is important to try to separate these two components of the self-concept, not least in order to trace how they interact.

Self-observations fall into two broad classes: there is self-observation in the strict sense, that is observation of one's own ideas, feelings, and perhaps especially behaviour; and observation of one's general situation, and one's place within it. We shall begin with the unemployed individual's view of his general situation, as the setting in which he observes himself as a person.

## The general situation

To recapitulate in order to avoid misunderstanding: we shall be primarily concerned with the literature on the kind of unemployed individual who has been in regular employment; in other words, we shall be mainly concerned with those whose assumption is (or had been) that they would 'normally' be in a job. Given this, there are consistent reports of two early reactions to becoming unemployed: first, on hearing of his impending unemployment, the individual is *aware* of a sense of shock; second, when the job has actually come to an end, there is frequently (though not universally) a sense that one is 'on holiday' (e.g. Hill, 1978; *not* so clear in Wedderburn, 1964; Briar, 1977; Swinburn, 1981). We have considered these phenomena already in our discussion of the 'stages' of unemployment (cf. p. 18ff). The sense of 'holiday', at least for a short time, is more explicit in accounts from the post-1945 period than in those of the thirties. This may reflect the better provision for the unemployed since the last war. It may also be relevant to recall, however, that the pre-war literature on unemployment only begins in the early thirties, after more than ten years of high levels of unemployment: to become unemployed in the thirties, given the history of the twenties, must therefore have been profoundly daunting; far more so than to become unemployed in the late sixties and early seventies, after two decades of full employment, and confidence in the availability of work. Whatever the reason, the psychologically significant point is that to see oneself as 'on holiday', even if only to give thought to one's future, implies that one does not yet identify oneself as 'unemployed'. The concept of 'holiday' is inherently a concept of the world of work: in effect, as long as an individual looks on himself as taking a holiday, he does not see or fully accept his situation as that of the 'unemployed'.

It would be very useful now if we were able to isolate the factors which bring the sense of holiday to an end. Unfortunately, as we noted when we discussed the 'stages of unemployment' the literature tells little, if anything, about the processes of transition between stages and these processes are by no means self-evident. This particular transition, for instance, cannot be simply attributed to the bureaucracy of welfare provision: that, in the form of 'signing on', begins immediately on loss of work. (We can, of course, base ourselves only on procedures which prevail in the United Kingdom; but then, the literature with which we are here concerned also relates mainly to this country.) All we can record, therefore, is that there comes a point when the unemployed individual no longer sees his situation as like a holiday, but recognises that he is indeed one of the 'unemployed'. Which comes first, the recognition that one is unemployed, or a different way of construing one's situation, is a tempting but useless question: these are two aspects of the same transformation. As the individual sees it, he is someone who has to 'sign on', usually queuing and waiting to go through the routines required for obtaining benefit. The procedures may have changed in important details over the years (see p. 32, above), but they are nevertheless resented today, just as they were in the thirties (Bakke, 1933; Pilgrims Trust, 1938; Gould and Kenyon, 1972; Marsden and Duff, 1975; Schlackman Research Organisation Ltd, 1978). That resentment, anger, frustration, make it clear that the unemployed individual sees his situation as humiliating. There is the standing or sitting around, simply waiting to be dealt with: there is the mixing with all kinds of other people in the dole queue, whom there is a marked tendency to look down upon (we shall return to this): and, psychologically most important of all, there is the profound invasion of privacy, by bureaucratic enquiries into one's financial position, family circumstances, relationships with cohabitants, and the like. There are aspects of his situation (only aspects), which are reminiscent of the de-individuating treatment of people in 'total institutions', such as hospitals (Goffman, 1961b; see also Dipboye, 1977). Objectively considered, 'society' may have some justification in making such enquiries, but they are fundamentally incursions on privacy which that same society is most jealous to guard in relation to its other members

(Kelvin, 1973). He may not put it in precisely these words, though some come close to it, but the unemployed individual sees his situation as essentially that of a second-class citizen (Gould and Kenyon, 1972; Marsden and Duff, 1975; Schlackman Research Organisation Ltd, 1978). There are also indications in several of the autobiographies and case histories, that some unemployed people are afraid of the bureaucracy, of authority – this may be perhaps especially so among those who in fact have little to hide, but whose past regular work has left them unprepared for second-class citizenship.

Granted that not everyone enters unemployment with a sense of taking 'a bit of a holiday', the difference between that initial approach and the recognition that one is unemployed constitutes a profound change in the perception of one's situation. The very essence of a 'holiday', as of leisure generally, is the sense that the situation, whatever it may be, is in one's own control: even if one sometimes seems to surrender this control – for instance, by going on some organised tour – that surrender was, and is admitted to have been, one's own choice, and can be reversed if one so chooses. Unemployment, of the involuntary kind with which we are here concerned, and its consequences, creates the sense of a situation largely out of one's control, especially in one's relations with the state. More generally, perceived internal locus of control at the beginning becomes perceived external locus of control, at least over certain areas of one's life; but to that we shall return later.

The literature also provides consistent evidence that unemployment reduces an individual's social life (and often his family's), and that he is much aware of this, often painfully so (e.g. Bakke, 1933; Komarovski, 1940; Gould and Kenyon, 1972; Marsden and Duff, 1975; Briar, 1977). There are several issues here, of which the most fundamental is the extent to which unemployed people are *ostracised* by others, or *withdraw themselves* from social activities. The complex problems of withdrawal from a sense of stigma, as well as of real and apparent ostracism, we shall leave until we discuss how the unemployed individual is seen, and perceives himself to be seen. For the present suffice it to say that although some withdrawal may indeed be due to a sense of shame at being unemployed, we would advise against attributing too much to the power of the Protestant Work Ethic (see pp. 100–9). There are quite earthy, but none the less important other factors. To be workless is to be cashless: to be cashless is to be unable to return hospitality; it is to be unable to take one's turn at buying drinks, let alone at 'entertaining'. The unemployeds' problem is not nearly so much the Protestant Ethic *à la* Weber (1905), as the Norm of Reciprocity *à la* Gouldner (1960). In a society rich in surpluses, especially of trivia, the giving and reciprocation of gifts has largely lost the symbolic psychological significance which it had and has in 'simpler' societies – except for those at the margin, for whom even a trifle received becomes a burden to repay. To participate without being able to reciprocate is to see oneself, and to feel, less than a whole man or woman (Bakke, 1933; and Marsden and Duff, 1975, cite particularly good examples of this feeling). There are, therefore, clear-cut practical grounds which, in conjunction with their social psychological effects, lead the unemployed to reduce or even to withdraw from much of their one-time social life. Unfortunately, this also creates the possibility that an unemployed individual may sometimes perceive his own essentially pre-emptive withdrawal as ostracism by other people: there are the makings here of self-fulfilling prophecy.

However, the problem is clearly not simply that of the self-consciousness of the unemployed individual, aware of being different from friends who are in work. Sometimes a whole community is hit by unemployment, and where this happens there is a marked decline of social and communal activities throughout it (Jahoda *et al.*, 1933/72; Pilgrim Trust, 1938; Sinfield, 1974). This cannot be explained in terms of the withdrawal of the unemployed individual from the social life of employed friends. Almost on the contrary: where unemployment is the common fate of a community, where in fact there are people who have the time, one might reasonably have assumed that communal activities would increase: yet, for example, the communal gardens of Marienthal, once the source of considerable village pride, were neglected, though there were many who could have tended them (Jahoda *et al.*, 1933/72). The withdrawal of the unemployed from social life cannot, therefore, be attributed solely to factors which are themselves social, such as a sense of being 'different', of having failed as a person, of being unable to reciprocate hospitality: such feelings may seem valid for an unemployed individual in a 'normal' working community, but not where that community as a whole is out of work. It also seems unlikely that two quite different sets of factors explain the reduction of social life in 'normal' and in unemployed communities. Consequently, while social factors, such as a sense of stigma, may indeed often be very relevant, two other factors may be even more basic: the sheer, progressively exhausting effort needed to keep going at all, just oneself and one's family; and, second, the unemployed individual's frequent debilitating dislike of himself, which we shall consider later.

There is one important exception to this typical pattern of withdrawal from social life. The literature with which we have been concerned has dealt with the effects of unemployment on the *adult* worker, the man or woman who has typically been in work for two or three years at least; this literature encompasses the 'young adult', but rarely touches on the special case of the unemployed school leaver or on youth unemployment generally. There is a very useful review of the social psychological literature on that topic by Carroll (1979). A basic complication is that very much depends on the family of the young unemployed (Milham *et al.*, 1978; Pahl and Wallace, 1980). A supportive family may greatly ease the problems of the young unemployed, a hostile one may make the teenage boy or girl feel even more rejected than an adult, because the adult at least usually has a 'home'. More generally, in our culture this is a gregarious age group: the literature which we have encountered in passing suggests that the young unemployed want for money much more than they want for friends: they do not see themselves as without friends, only as limited in the extent to which they can join in activities which need cash.

We return to the 'typical' unemployed individual, the one who is 'adult', has normally been regularly employed, and who is tacitly but very generally assumed to be married and to have a family. So far we have considered only those aspects of his situation which are a product of unemployment as such, that is, the day-to-day characteristics of being unemployed. To reach a more rounded understanding and explanation of the effects of being unemployed, it is also essential to look at what an individual *loses*, psychologically, through not being at work. This issue was raised very forcefully by Jahoda in 1979, and it has in fact been a recurrent theme in the literature since its earliest days – though it was often expressed in 'moral' rather than 'psychological' language (e.g. Beveridge, 1909/31; Jahoda *et al.*, 1933/72; Pilgrim Trust, 1938). In the present context the underlying assumption is that the way in which an unemployed individual sees his immediate situation must include, however inarticulately, the contrast with his situation while he was in work: that contrast is particularly marked in terms of its social psychological characteristics. Unemployment brings a loosening and disintegration of a number of previously crucial fixed points in the individual's social environment. The most obvious of these are the loss of an active occupational role, and the fading of many job-related friendships; less tangibly, but none the less disturbingly, there is a general sense of loss of status; and beyond this, the individual may come to doubt whether he can still truly claim to belong to work-related organisations such as a particular trade union or professional association, which may once have been an important reference group.

Although loss of one's active occupational role is the most immediate, blatant, and concrete consequence of becoming unemployed, the psychological literature on unemployment only refers to this, it does not seem to have explored its implications. In a sense this is understandable: the substantial literature on the work role as such belongs to industrial, occupational, and organisational psychology (cf. Katz and Kahn, 1978;

Brown, 1978) Yet unless those of us who study unemployment consider at least the basic psychological characteristics of the work role, we cannot adequately account for the effects of losing it. We ourselves cannot here supply what is missing but we can at least begin to identify the problems. There may be important connections between an individual's one-time work, as such, and his (or her) reaction to becoming and being unemployed: we have not, however, found any study which has systematically explored this relationship. The most that we have are occasional, fleeting glimpses of unemployed skilled men pursuing skilled activities in garden sheds, of salesmen setting out to sell themselves, of managers making an office of their dining-room to manage their search for work, and so on (Marsden and Duff, 1975; Wedderburn, 1964; Swinburn, 1981).

There are therefore hints that at least at the outset some people may tackle their unemployment much as they tackled their jobs. On judgement this seems more plausible for some occupations than for others, but we do not know: nor do we know for how long such a carry-over persists, nor to what extent it is helpful or, in fact, a barrier to adjustment. Inasmuch as it occurs it is, presumably, a transfer of skills. It is, however, also a means of seeing one's situation as fundamentally unchanged, and of maintaining important aspects of the self-concept which had been based on one's job. Except that when one is unemployed there are no role partners in one's activities; there is therefore little, if any, social reinforcement of one's role, only a growing realisation that one is on one's own; and ultimately there may come a sense that one is simply playing games. Much of this is inevitably conjecture, which is why there is need for research: for the capacity to cope with unemployment, or some of the problems of coping with it, may well be related to the individual's one-time job, and to the nature and significance of that job, as such, to his self-concept.

More generally, the essential psychological feature of the work role is that it *locates* the individual in a network of relationships with others: in his work role he has a defined place and function within a social system. Note that from our general social psychological standpoint it is irrelevant that a given individual in a given position within that system may regard himself as in an ambiguous situation, may experience role conflict, or role strain, as in the classic studies of Killian, 1952; Gross *et al.*, 1958, and numerous others (cf. McLean, 1974). Though its psychological consequences may well be serious, role ambiguity, role strain, role conflict, are essentially administrative problems. The fundamental fact is that these problems only arise for the individual precisely because he is an integral part of a system of relationships. He is part of a system of expectations: he sees himself as entitled to hold expectations of others and, within the system, he and his activities are defined by the expectations which others in turn have of him. We shall not continue to labour the issue, but established work-role relationships constitute a clear case of the operation, in a social context, of the complex 'internal' processes of schemata. We need merely add that since in most instances an individual's job covers a very substantial proportion of his daily life, the schemata related to the job equally cover much of that life.

Conversely losing one's regular job removes one from a previously stable system of relationships, and renders invalid the sets of expectations and patterns of behaviour associated with it. The literature on unemployment is basically quite inadequate on this issue. Readers acquainted with the literature may be surprised by this judgement, but it arises from the need to distinguish between the *formal* and *informal* social aspects of losing one's job. From the earliest studies to those of our time, accounts of the consequences of unemployment repeatedly report the sense of loss of the informal socialising at work, of the loss of its camaraderie (Bakke, 1933). For the record the Austrian women of *Marienthal* missed this companionship in the thirties just as much as the British men in our own time (Jahoda *et al.*, 1933/72; Gould and Kenyon, 1972; Marsden and Duff, 1975; Hill, 1978). None of this is in dispute: and it is not the point at issue. That point is that as long *as an individual is in a job he is, by virtue of his work alone, part of a structure of social relationships.* It is inherent in the nature of almost all work that the work of one individual is integrated with that of others – and if it is to get done he has to interact with them in terms of their work-role relationships with him. The set of people who are his role partners on the job may indeed largely overlap with the set of his social contacts outside it, but the two sets do not inevitably coincide. Furthermore, even when some particular person does belong to both sets, his standing in one, as a hard worker, for example, may be very different from his standing in the other, as a friend. It is therefore necessary to assume that the social environment of an individual's job gives rise to two separate, only partly overlapping aspects of his self-concept: one derived from the formal relationships of his work role, the other from informal relationships with friends at work.

Once an individual has been out of work for a little while, he may, in retrospect, recall especially the informal camaraderie of the factory, or office, or whatever the work-place. Though there will be much truth in what he recalls, it may also be exaggerated. As we have seen, unemployment leads to a cutting back and often a very positive withdrawal from social life (Jahoda *et al.*, 1933/72; Komarovsky, 1940; Briar, 1977): consequently, in response to the questions of researchers, or just in telling his story, the sense of his (or her) current isolation may lead the unemployed individual to romanticise the work-place: While at work, however, it must be assumed that strictly *work*-related activities occupy a substantial proportion of time and social interactions; and there is no reason to think that these are inherently less salient merely because they are work related. On the contrary, the sense of belonging to a working group, structured by its functions, is itself psychologically significant, and not least to the individual's self-concept as having a rightful place in a purposive group:

'the next time you see a *lot of fellows* standing and watching a *gang* laying a pavement or putting up a house, just ask yourself how much fun it is to stand and watch other men work'.                    (Bakke, 1933, pp. 63–4: our italics)

There is psychologically a great deal of difference between being one among a random lot of isolated 'fellows' and being a member of a 'gang'.

We do not wish to be sentimental about work: working groups, and relations within them, are by no means always and constant sources of unalloyed joy. Nevertheless, at the lowest level of the sheer amount of life taken by work, an individual's work role must constitute a very pervasive component of his self-concept. The fact that work-role relationships are functional – and not just friendly social chat – also provides the individual with the sense that he himself has a function, a function which gives him a place within a social structure. There is a hint about the importance about having some such 'place' in the careful longitudinal study of unemployment by Kasl and his colleagues (Kasl, 1975; Kasl *et al.*, 1975; Gore, 1978). They drew their samples of unemployed men from factories whose processes were comparable, but which were located in either an urban or a rural setting. Workers who were made redundant in rural areas (after years of regular work) showed consistently less stress than similar workers made redundant in the city. The authors suggest that a rural setting may provide the individual with more social support than an urban one. There is a confounding factor here, in that the rural setting was also homogeneous in terms of minority ethnic origin (Polish). Even so, there is a possible implication in these findings which deserves further attention: in a large sprawling urban area, the work-place may itself be the most distinctive 'community' of which the individual can feel himself to be a member; in a small country place, the individual may feel more readily that he belongs to a community which exists in its own right, independently of his work. The position is, of course, not quite so simple: as we have seen, when the whole community is hit by unemployment, as in *Marienthal*, or in some English and Welsh villages of the thirties (Pilgrim Trust, 1938), there is a marked decline in all social and communal life: under such circumstances there may be not enough of a 'community' to give support to stricken individuals. Another complication is evidence from the United

States that rural areas may be more hostile to their unemployed (Williamson, 1974; Osgood, 1977); the unemployed in these instances may, however, have been relatively isolated individuals or groups in their localities, and fairly 'visible' in a rural setting. Taken together, these various findings suggest that there may be an optimal level of unemployment for any one community, such that the community is still economically and socially viable, yet its unemployed are too numerous to be all dismissed as lay-abouts; the community may then have both the resources and the will to support its jobless. That, however, is a matter for further research.

In principle, the most obvious source of stable relationships and support in our society is, of course, an individual's family (assuming he or she has one); and this is also potentially a very important source of a sense of personal significance. However, the general situation of the family is itself inevitably affected by the unemployment of one (or more) of its members. As regards marriage, the consensus of evidence is that unemployment increases tensions between husband and wife, and that this *may* bring to breaking-point relationships which were already fragile: but that, in other instances, marriage and family life gain a greater sense of general closeness through the very difficulties of unemployment, and despite its undoubted particular stresses (Komarovsky, 1940; Briar, 1977). Much depends on how a family copes with the sheer problems of being with one another far more often and for far longer stretches of time. The basic findings, though inconclusive, seem to have been consistent across the years: the frustrations and tensions of being unemployed add to, rather than change, the fundamental patterns of pre-existing relationships – destroying those already waiting for destruction and reinforcing bonds already strong in countering a common adversity (Jahoda *et al.*, 1933/72; Komarovsky, 1940; Marsden and Duff, 1975; Fagin, 1980). An individual's concept of himself-in-his-marriage, whatever the quality of that marriage, may be enhanced by the experiences of unemployment, but it is rarely fundamentally transformed by it (Jahoda *et al.*, 1933/72; Komarovsky, 1940; Marsden and Duff, 1975):

Particularly distressing for many men is the change which they see in their situation *vis-à-vis* their children. They have a sense that they have failed their children, and that they have lost status and authority in their children's eyes. Occasionally there is also deep bitterness at what is perceived to be loss of love and affection through loss of income, through not being able to supply pocket-money, presents, luxuries. Much the most detailed accounts and analyses which we have found are still those of Komarovsky (1940). As in the relationship between the unemployed man and his wife, so in his relationship with his children, much depended on how a father had got on with his children before he became unemployed. As a cautious generalisation, the fathers of Komarovsky's study had perhaps more problems with their adolescent off-spring than with children under twelve; but they might well have had problems with their teenagers in any case. There are two issues here, not only in Komarovsky's American research of the thirties, but also in much more recent studies in the United Kingdom of the seventies (Marsden and Duff, 1975; Fagin, 1980). First, unemployment induces a feeling that one has failed in the role of father-as-breadwinner, as provider of the strictly *material* needs of the household: and inasmuch as a man's status and authority in his family derive from his role as provider – or are perceived by him to derive from this – then unemployment does indeed undermine the legitimacy of his claim to them – at least as he now sees himself. Secondly, and more subtly, the unemployed father also often feels that he has let down his family *socially*, that he degrades it by being unemployed. This fear of 'contaminating' the rest of the family seems to be especially marked in connection with children at school, and with older teenagers just beginning to have social lives of their own. The fact is that the fathers are to some extent justified in their fear and consequent sense of guilt; it is clear that the children of unemployed parents do frequently feel stigmatised by their poverty, and that there is a sufficient number of sufficiently nasty children of working parents who stigmatise the children of the unemployed. The sad practical consequence is that (in the United Kingdom) parents will, for instance, forego provisions such as free school meals for their children, to avoid the children from being exposed to taunts (Marsden and Duff, 1975; Hill, 1978; Schlackman Research Organisation Ltd, 1978).

Where the man is also the 'head' of the household and its principal breadwinner, the literature leaves little doubt that his unemployment usually affects his relationship with wife and children. This may be valid as a generalisation, but needs to be treated with care. We have already noted that unemployment normally only intensifies pre-existing patterns of relations, heightening problems in some cases but also tightening bonds in others. From a strictly social psychological standpoint there has to be an even more fundamental proviso. An individual's self-concept in the context of his marriage or as a parent will presumably be much influenced by the concepts of 'marriage' and of 'parenthood' (and 'fatherhood') in his *culture* or *sub-culture*. There are hints of a recognition of this in the Pilgrim Trust's brief comparison of the effects of unemployment on marriage in Welsh and Durham villages and in Liverpool (Pilgrim Trust, 1938), and in Oeser on unemployment in Dundee (Oeser, 1937); and there is also an implicit recognition of cultural factors in Komarovsky's deliberately homogeneous sampling of white Protestant families (Komarovsky, 1940), and more explicitly in Triandis' work on the hard-core unemployed (Triandis *et al.*, 1975; see also Feldman, 1973a, b). However, the problem does not seem to have received attention from research in its own right – although it must be assumed that the concept of 'marriage' and of 'father', whether as an aspect of religious faith, or of local history, or of both, may significantly modify the effects of unemployment upon it.

It is important to consider the situation from another perspective. Much has been said and written on how unemployment heightens family tensions and problems: turned around, and perhaps especially as seen by the unemployed, love and responsibilities for a family greatly heighten the problems of unemployment, particularly the financial ones. On the one hand the family man is often very painfully aware of the deprivation which his unemployment has brought to his wife and children; on the other, in some cases in the United Kingdom, the social security benefits available to a man with a family may occasionally equal or exceed what he could expect to earn from such work as might be open to him (Daniel, 1974a; recent evidence shows that this is very rare: it arises almost exclusively among low-paid workers with three or more dependent children. Davies *et al.*, 1982). In either case, the family man is likely to be more aware of his economic situation than someone unattached – if only because his situation is likely to be more complex.

There is, of course, a large literature on poverty (Townsend, 1974; Field, 1977a, b), and the poor include most of the unemployed, especially the long-term unemployed. There appears to be very little information, however, on the 'domestic economy' of the kind of unemployed individual who has 'normally' been in work; and there seems to be even less on how such an individual perceives his domestic economy. As we have already noted, he often has a sense of no longer being able to afford a full social life. More generally, the literature abounds with references to the reduced circumstances of the unemployed; and autobiographies and case histories repeatedly reveal how very much the unemployed are aware of this (Jahoda *et al.*, 1933/72; Briar, 1977; Swinburn, 1981). It seems obvious to common sense that this should be so, and in some respects common sense is correct. Nevertheless there is a problem here. The evidence stems almost wholly from people who had already been unemployed for some time before it was collected: by that time they had become very conscious of their relative, and often absolute, poverty. However, it is reasonable to assume, and some of the case studies confirm it, that anyone who has been regularly employed enters unemployment with at least some resources, with a stock, and even 'reserves', in terms of clothes, shoes, and basics of that kind. In most such cases, the economic consequences of becoming unemployed therefore develop only over several weeks and months. Yet even where we do have some information on these first few weeks or months (e.g. Bakke, 1933; Wedderburn, 1964; Marsden and Duff, 1975; Kasl *et al.*, 1975; Swinburn, 1981) it offers no more than incidental and scattered glimpses of how the *recently* unemployed see their economic situation. Though there have, of course, been numerous studies of the household incomes of the unemployed (Jahoda *et al.*, 1933/72; Pilgrim Trust, 1938; Daniel, 1974a; Briar, 1977; Hawkins, 1979; Davies *et al.*, 1982) there still seems to be only one which tried to trace *systematic* relationships between declining household resources and the general attitudes to life of the unemployed: that was by Jahoda and her colleagues in the Marienthal of 1931. Even at this time, the condition of the unemployed in Britain was considerably better (Bakke, 1933; Pilgrim Trust, 1938), and provision for the unemployed has much improved since, both in the United Kingdom and elsewhere (Jahoda, 1979b). Consequently, evidence from the thirties, or more recent evidence derived from people who have been unemployed for many months, is inadequate and possibly misleading: it obscures that the rate of strictly economic decline on becoming unemployed may be relatively slow, especially where an individual had previously been in steady regular work. Eventually cars have to be sold, telephones given up, and clothes get shabby (Briar, 1977). This does not, however, happen all at once, and what happens in the course of the decline may be much influenced by psychological factors, as well as by purely economic ones. For example, it may be that economic necessity imposes from the outset constraints which depress the individual; but it could also be that he becomes so depressed by his situation and perceived prospects that he makes excessive economies, which then depress him even further. There will, no doubt, be individual differences in this respect – which is precisely why the issue is not merely of academic interest but directly relevant to counselling the unemployed. Briar, for instance, notes that giving up the telephone may seriously reduce chances of finding work; depressed and self-reinforcing misperception of one's economic situation may thus lead to economies which look 'sensible', but are in fact self-defeating.

The few studies which have encompassed the onset of unemployment at best provide only hints of the perception of the situation at that stage. Wedderburn (1964), for example, found weekly paid workers to be more concerned to find work quickly than monthly paid men: there is therefore indirect evidence of different initial levels of anxiety on entering unemployment (or the mere prospect of becoming unemployed). In the event 48% of her sample moved immediately from one job to another – this was in the early 1960s – and altogether 84% had found work within a month (Wedderburn, 1964): inevitably, there is no detailed account of how they coped with the economic consequences of unemployment. More recently, Swinburn (1981) reported briefly on the perception of their financial situation of unemployed managers and professional staff. This small sample covered a slightly longer period. There was no evidence as yet of hardship, but there was clearly much concern, and there was evidence, though mainly indirect, of the careful assessment and reassessment of priorities, and of self-consciously careful planning.

At the other end of the socio-economic scale, the demography of unemployment has consistently shown that some groups of workers are much more likely to become unemployed than others, and first among these are the unskilled, who are often also low paid even when they have work (Daniel, 1974a; Sinfield, 1981). This was again confirmed by a recent, detailed analysis of the incomes of the unemployed: of those who had remained unemployed after three months, one-third had also been in the bottom tenth of the earnings distribution even when in work; furthermore – and perhaps itself worth psychological enquiry – 'among the married men no more than one third had a wife in employment, a proportion far below the 60% found in the working population as a whole' (Davies *et al.*, 1982, p. 239). The 'reserves' of this most vulnerable group are therefore likely to be very limited, and the effects on them of becoming unemployed may therefore set in fairly quickly.

For our present considerations, however, the most important finding of this analysis is the sheer *range* of the drop in incomes represented by the discrepancies between earlier earnings and unemployment benefits: 12% had dropped by more than £50 per week; 18% between £30–50; 19% between £20–30; 27% between £10–20: for the record *only* 6% received *more* in benefits, only 1% by more than £10 (Davies *et al.*, 1982, table 1, p. 240. These figures are based on 976 cases of a 1978 cohort. To gauge the real value of these drops at 1982 levels, the 1982 equivalent of a £40 per week drop would be £70). There are thus huge variations in the initial economic circumstances, and in the extent of the subsequent relative economic decline of the unemployed. It must be assumed that such marked differences in their economic background and conditions will affect the reactions of individuals, and of whole households, to the experience of unemployment; indeed, if they do *not* have significant effects, that itself would have to be established and explained. Yet for all practical purposes psychological research on unemployment has ignored these factors. Inasmuch as it touches on the domestic economy of the unemployed at all, it paints portraits, often very moving portraits, of poverty firmly established, and of its miseries: but with the one exception of *Marienthal*, we have not found any attempt to explore systematically the *interaction* of economic and psychological changes induced by unemployment.

So far we have considered the situation of the unemployed individual in terms of the consequences for the micro-economy of the household: in essence this is concerned with the unemployed as a consumer, as it were a much restricted, an increasingly constrained consumer. The unemployed individual also reacts to his position at a macro-economic level, namely when he looks at his prospects as a worker. In that context, a number of studies have drawn attention to the phenomenon of the 'discouraged worker' – the unemployed individual who sees himself as so unlikely to find work that he withdraws himself from the labour market altogether. In essence the discouraged worker is someone who for one or more of a variety of reasons is at the margin of the work-force, and then falls outside it when there is a decline in economic activity. Examples are people with disabilities or recurrent ailments, older workers, the unskilled, married women. The phenomenon has been considered in a number of articles (Flaim, 1973; Hill *et al.*, 1973; Daniel and Stilgoe, 1977) and commends itself intuitively. There are however two problems in this connection which deserve more rigorous enquiry. First, the phenomenon of the discouraged worker is obviously a product of the operation of subjective probabilities. It is important to establish the factors which determine these probabilities, especially in relation to objective probabilities. We know that there is a link, because the incidence of discouraged workers varies with local levels of unemployment. Daniel, for instance, has shown that the perceived prospects of finding employment in a given locality affect the way in which people perceive their handicaps, illnesses, and personal problems: the *same kind of handicap* which often leads an individual to see himself as 'disabled' in an area of high unemployment, and therefore to withdraw himself from the work-force, is simply taken for granted, and ignored as 'just a fact of life' by workers (and, presumably also *employers*) in areas where unemployment is low. The second problem is related to this. Economies also improve, which should give rise to the 'encouraged worker'. The tacit assumption of the potentially encouraged worker underlies numerous theories and schemes for training the long-term or 'hard-core' unemployed (Hutson and Smith, 1969; Morgan *et al.*, 1970; Rosenquist, 1972; Beatty, 1974; Triandis *et al.*, 1974; Campling, 1978): indeed one sad little study by O'Leary (1972) shows that encouragement may so raise confidence and expectations that 'successful' trainees apply for unrealistically 'better' jobs than they are objectively likely to get. Our main concern, however, is the essentially 'ordinary' worker who has become unemployed. We know that he becomes discouraged, but little of the factors, and the time-lags, of his becoming so: we know even less of the factors which would *en*courage him or her to come back into the work-force after having been discouraged. Financial considerations are, of course, likely to be 'relevant', but they are neither necessary nor sufficient – for to be discouraged is to be resigned to failure, and to feel helpless about it.

The chances are that most readers will not even have noticed that all we have said so far has been essentially based on, and referred to, the situation of the unemployed *man*: we have found scarcely any research on the unemployed *woman*. There are exceptions to this in relation to exceptional problems, such as research on the training of hard-core unemployed black women in the United States (O'Leary, 1972; see also Seiden, 1976). For all practical purposes, however, though women do feature in the literature of unemployment, they do so first and foremost as the wives of unemployed men, and as the mothers of such men's children. Their situation is considered almost exclusively in terms of their indeed crucial role in the family: it is very very rare that they are given attention as unemployed workers in their own right. To be more precise: one occasionally finds references to unemployed *single* women, or women who are on their own (e.g. Pilgrim Trust, 1938; Gould and Kenyon, 1972; Hill, 1978). However, even when one finds that needle in a haystack, a reference to an unemployed married woman, the frame of reference remains that of the housewife:

Nearly all the accounts of their lives mention the fact that their housework used to keep them up late into the night after a day at the factory. But nearly all of these accounts also contain a sentence such as this: 'If only we could get back to work.' ... it is not merely because of the money: ... The factory widened their sphere of existence and provided them with social contacts which they now miss. (Jahoda *et al.*, 1933/72, pp. 76–7)

For a married woman, housework has to be carried on; and it continues to be seen as her principal task. Work, in the sense of 'a job', is still regarded as somehow secondary for a married woman: it is seen to come second to looking after the home; and it is second also in status, as a source of income which is 'additional' to the earnings of the husband (Sinfield, 1981). Sinfield records, furthermore, that

Many wives have stressed to me in interviews that it is not right for a woman to go out to work when her husband is unemployed ... These informal pressures are so strong that many women wait until the husband has found work before starting work themselves. (Sinfield, 1981, p. 87)

This is no more than a recent confirmation from the woman's side of a theme which forms a steady undercurrent in interviews with unemployed men: somehow 'it isn't right' for the woman to be the breadwinner; somehow it unmans the man (Marsden and Duff, 1975; Briar, 1977). Sinfield's comments on the pressures on women may help to explain the findings of Davies *et al.* (1982) which we reported earlier: among unemployed married men only about one-third had wives who held a job, compared with 60% of men with working wives in the working population as a whole. If one looks only at Davies' statistics, one's impression might well be that the unemployed household is 'typically' inadequate: neither the husband nor the wife, it would appear, has much to offer as a worker; or they cannot settle down to a job; or they just cannot be bothered to work. If, however, there is a substantial proportion of wives who feel that they cannot 'do it' to their man to go to work while he stays at home unemployed, the nature of the problem changes: it becomes not the problem of the basic inadequacy of people, but of the persistence of a tradition which has so outlived itself that it destroys the very qualities it once encouraged. Quite apart from the economic nonsense of the wife's self-inflicted unemployment, it is a tragic irony at a personal level: the underlying motive is the maintenance of the family and its structure; yet we know that one of the most destructive effects of unemployment is the increasing tension between husband and wife, confined day in and day out to the home and to each other's company.

Far too little is known about the unemployed woman to delineate how she is likely to perceive her situation. There is evidence of single women, proud of the independence they had had when in work, and anxious to retain it in their unemployment (Pilgrim Trust, 1938; Fraser, 1969). However, although the independence provided by her job may be very significant for a woman (and not only for a single woman but perhaps also for many married ones), unemployment does not seem to induce in a woman a sense of *failure-as-a-woman*, in the way in which it so frequently seems to produce a sense of *failure-as-a-man* among men. In terms of the underlying social psychological processes involved, 'having a job' does not appear to be as integral to the *social reality* of women as of men; it does not appear to be as integral to the *social representation*, to the concept of 'woman' as of 'man' in our society; and it is therefore probably not as dominant a theme in the *socialisation* of girls as of boys: *not* to have a job is therefore also likely to be less salient in the *social comparison processes* of women than of men, at least in relation to other women (Festinger, 1954; Berger and Luckman, 1967). These gender-related differences may be changing, but an historical perspective suggests that the change is to be measured in generations and decades, rather than in years. Even if we ignore that women have worked in agriculture and in domestic employment from time immemorial (and were not unknown to work in mines), they have from its beginnings worked in manufacturing industry; certainly since the 1914–18 war they have worked in industries which had once been the 'preserve' of men, and a recurrent complaint of unemployed men in the 1930s was that women had taken their jobs

(Bakke, 1933; see also Hawkins, 1979). At a purely quantitative level, at the end of 1981 women accounted for over 40% of the employed work-force of Great Britain: and while unemployment overall had doubled between late 1977 (6.33%) and the end of 1981 (12.58%), the proportion of women in the active work-force rose slightly, from 40.9% to 42.25%. Nevertheless, although it is clearly central to the (British) economy that women hold jobs, to hold a job still does not appear to be as central to the social psychological situation of a woman as of a man. The unemployed woman may be as socially isolated, bored, frustrated, anxious, and poor as the unemployed man; if she is married and her unemployment is self-inflicted to protect the ego of her man, she may see her situation as even more complicated and frustrating than his; but she is much less likely to see her situation as personally deeply demeaning.

All this is no more than conjecture, suggested by fragments of inciden-tal evidence. We know of several current research projects which are specifically concerned with the situation and reactions of unemployed women, and these will help to clarify issues which we can only suspect: as of now (early 1980s), however, the literature is essentially that of the *unemployed man*.

### Self-observation

Here we shall be concerned with the self-descriptive accounts of the unemployed. Almost all psychological and sociological studies of the unemployed include examples of their observations and comments on themselves. To these have to be added collections of autobiographical accounts, such as Beales and Lambert (1934), and Gould and Kenyon (1972), and reports in the press and broadcasting media. Some of this material we have considered already. We noted in the previous section that some unemployed, for instance skilled men, undertake jobs at home which use their skills; others, for example those with managerial or sales experience, set up an 'office' in the home, to 'manage' their search for work. There is good evidence that an important and quite conscious function of this strategy is to be able to continue to see oneself doing the kind of work with which one had identified (Marsden and Duff, 1975; Briar, 1977; Swinburn, 1981).

Sooner or later, however, and mostly perhaps quite soon, the unem-ployed individual becomes deeply aware of his seemingly unending amount of free time. Naturally there are exceptions to any such generalis-ation: occasionally there is evidence of individuals for whom unemploy-ment provided a positive and welcome opportunity to develop interests and activities – but this seems to be rare. Much the dominant theme is of an almost obsessive preoccupation with time – with the extent of it, with the inability to make use of it, with the sense that one is therefore merely 'killing' it. From the early thirties to the present day, research on unemployment has consistently documented the consciousness of the unemployed of the emptiness of their days (e.g. Jahoda *et al.*, 1933/72; Komarovsky, 1940; Marsden and Duff, 1975; Briar, 1977; Hill, 1978).

This is far more than a purely rational recognition of objective fact; it has behavioural and emotional consequences, of which the unemployed are themselves fully aware. The lack of demands on one's time means that much of one's day-to-day existence is unstructured. As a result, a lassitude sets in, so that in Marienthal, for example, men walked at a markedly slowed pace; unemployment had induced an overall lowering of 'tone', physical as well as psychological; and it is clear from the comments and diaries of these people that they were conscious of their deterioration (Jahoda *et al.*, 1933/72). No other research since has provided an equally imaginative and yet detailed account, but the same basic pattern is evident in some of Bakke's quotations, and in his description of street-corner loafing in Greenwich; it is reflected in the Pilgrim's Trust's (1938) reports of demoralised people who stay in bed because they feel that there is nothing for which to get up. From our own time, some of the cases of Marsden and Duff (1975), and especially of Hill (1978), tell much the same story: and although it had not happened to them yet, Swinburn's (1981) sample of unemployed managers and professionals – sophisticated, resourceful and, not least, only recently unemployed – were openly conscious of a very real danger of deteriorating, unless they created strict demands for themselves.

Frequently bored and frustrated, the unemployed individual is a problem to others as well as to himself; and he knows it. We have deliberately said 'he', because this may be much more often a problem of unemployed men than of unemployed women. Certainly, the man sitting or hanging aimlessly around the house was a very serious source of tension in the classic study of Komarovsky (1940), and similar tensions are evident in other accounts of the 'unemployed family' (Marsden and Duff, 1975; Briar, 1977 – but note, this is not universal and inevitable – Fagin, 1980). The chances are that much the same kind of boredom and frustration may overtake the single woman, with much the same effects, if she is living with her family – say an unemployed daughter or sister: there are hints to that in occasional case studies (Hill, 1978). For a married woman, however, or for that matter for any woman who runs a household, the problem is usually rather different: it is not that she has nothing to do; on the contrary, she often has more to do under more difficult circumstances: but she may see herself as confined and deprived of a life, especially of a social life, of her own (Jahoda *et al.*, 1933/72; by implication, Seiden, 1976). Unfortunately, the literature on unemployed women is so meagre that these remarks should be considered more as hypotheses than as findings. Returning to men, therefore, it is clear that the unemployed man not only sees himself as bored and frustrated, but that seeing himself like that (as well as actually being so) also makes him irritable. This irritability becomes a regular feature of the day-to-day behaviour of the unemployed man: he is usually fully aware of it; it is talked about quite freely, both by unemployed men themselves and, where we know of them, by their families (Komarovsky, 1940; Marsden and Duff, 1975). In lay terms, such as 'he's a changed man', it is regarded as a change of personality; and although both the unemployed man and his family attribute the change to his situation, the unemployed man dislikes himself for it.

Feeling shut away at home is one of the most frequent complaints of the unemployed, and their own most frequent explanation of their irritability. From a psychological standpoint there are also other explanations, such as the disorienting effects of becoming unemployed; the consequent need to reappraise a host of things which one had previously taken for granted; and the doubts and anxieties engendered by these reappraisals, especially as there seems to be no end to the time one could spend mulling over them. We thus have an individual who is psychologically cooped up in his problems and physically cooped up in his home – the two probably enhancing each other.

There is one minor but striking difference in detail between the reports of the thirties and the seventies which may be of relevance in this context. The great killer of time for the unemployed of the seventies and eighties is almost certainly television (e.g. Hill, 1978). No single palliative of the thirties appears to have been equally pervasive and obliterating: radio was either not as widely available or not as mesmerising. At one level, of course, the fact that the unemployed now generally seem to have access to television reflects the significant improvement in their material condition. From a psychological standpoint the position is more complicated. The unemployed individual who incessantly watches television gets sick of doing so, and even sicker at seeing himself doing it; he is aware that he is merely killing time, and angry, and not least with himself, that he can find no better use for it.

The thirties did not have television, but they were a great period of the cinema: Bakke (1933) identified regular (and possibly quite frequent) visits to the cinema as a means of escape for the unemployed. Consider the differences: a 'regular' visit to the cinema, like any other regular 'event', rather than the constant background of television, gave a structure to the week (Mondays 'signing on', Wednesdays 'the pictures'); to go to the cinema was an 'occasion', where television is merely part of a daily drabness. Above all, going to the cinema meant getting out, and in two very important senses. First, it took one quite literally out of the home and amongst people, a relief from being cooped up. Secondly, it took one 'out of oneself' because, apart from brief news-reels, the cinema provided fantasy. Television brings the world into the home: a world which, as presented on television, is on the one hand depressing and fearsome, or, on the other, full of enticing goods, and services, and life styles which the unemployed cannot afford. To go to the cinema was (and where it occurs still is) to see oneself as doing something positive, akin, as it were, to taking a tonic: to sit at home, increasingly bored by television, is to see oneself as taking a drug, more or less aware of its increasingly debilitating side-effects.

It has to be said that there are no quantitative data on this. There will have been many people in the thirties who were too poor to go to the cinema (see Pilgrim Trust, 1938, on poverty): nowadays there may come a time when the television set also has to be sacrificed. Allowing for this, when one nevertheless looks at what is involved in going to the cinema and in watching television, the differences suggest the need for research into the *nature of the effects of television on the unemployed*, beyond the mere counting of the amount of time they spend on it.

To an outside observer it would seem that the unemployed individual could counter his sense of aimlessness by becoming involved in leisure activities or, ignoring legal niceties, by engaging in the 'informal' or even 'black' economy. The literature on this is very scanty. As regards *leisure*, we have already seen that reports from the thirties tell of a general decline in social and communal activity (Jahoda *et al.*, 1933/72; Pilgrim Trust, 1938). Bakke (1933) suggested, but could not provide direct evidence, that the skilled might have more personal and material resources to occupy themselves than the unskilled, and there is some support for this in the accounts of the skilled men in Marsden and Duff (1975). Fundamentally, however, the literature, such as it is, is much more given to preaching the need to educate people for leisure than to pursuing research into its nature and problems (Melching and Broberg, 1974; Spreitzer and Snyder, 1974; Brighthill and Mobley, 1977. There are more penetrating contributions: Parker, 1971; Jenkins and Sherman, 1981; Roberts, 1981).

The informal economy is a more complex matter. Though informal economic activities may have co-existed with formal economies from the beginning of time, it seems to be only quite recently that the 'informal economy' has been formulated as a concept, and thus identified as a domain for systematic research: as far as we can tell, this domain has not yet been explored from an explicitly psychological standpoint. It is, however, a potentially important field of study for social psychologists, not only in relation to unemployment but also in relation to work, para-economic activities such as moonlighting, and to sub-cultures within a society.

From Northern Ireland, for example, we have a brief but vivid account of the informal economy at work, two features of which are especially relevant to our concerns. First, the account shows very clearly the importance to an informal economy of the networks of accessible family, friends, and their connections. Secondly, it demonstrates that the gains from this activity are not only economic, and the non-economic ones benefit the 'employer' as well as the 'employee':

there is a social payoff for the employer, too, who is seen to do his duty by his relatives and friends ... the economic attractions (for the employee) are reinforced by the payoff in terms of one's social relationships with family and friends.                                         (Jenkins, 1978, p. 121)

The economic and social history of Northern Ireland may of course have created a community which is singularly sympathetic to informal economic activity. It is therefore important to remain cautious. Occasional references to it in other case studies suggest that informal economic activity may not be fully internalised (Marsden and Duff, 1975): it may help the individual financially; it may at times give him a certain immediate satisfaction; but it has, and is seen to have, an ephemeral quality, with less salience than a 'real' job or a 'pure' hobby.

There may therefore be a lower limit of regularity of employment, and of the time spent at it, below which the individual does not see himself sufficiently involved to incorporate it into his self-concept: and informal economic activity, perhaps especially of the 'black' variety, may often be too *ad hoc,* and of too short a duration, to rise above that limit. However, this cannot be the whole story. There are numerous occupations in the formal economy where employment is also haphazard and comes in short spells rather than long stretches, yet there is no reason to think that these are less important to the self-concepts of those who follow them than any other work: obvious examples are acting, music, the entertainment industry generally, freelance journalism, the many different trades of the ubiquitous independent 'little man'. At a strictly behavioural level therefore – that is, in terms of what the people concerned would observe and describe themselves as doing – employment in the informal economy is certainly not inherently different in nature and pattern from employment in the formal. As with leisure, so with informal economic activities: it is neither the nature of an activity which sets it apart from 'work', nor the fact that it may be intermittent; just as one man's job may be another's pastime, so it may be a third one's informal economic resource. In terms of observable behaviour, the boundaries between activities are often very tenuous.

In principle, therefore, an unemployed individual who engages in informal economic activity would observe himself doing, and could describe his various doings, much as would someone who did the same things for his normal living; much the same would be true of the pursuit of a host of leisure activities, though the monetary reward might be lacking – and even that not necessarily. In practice, however, the unemployed individual seems to be first and foremost conscious of what he is *not* doing: the case studies, for example, repeatedly record how the unemployed describe their lives as 'wasted': wasted because they cannot find the work for which they feel they are qualified. The sense of waste of one's life presumably develops only over time. There are, of course, the 'discouraged workers', who feel defeated about finding work as soon as they lose the job they have: 'older' workers, say in their fifties, may well feel like that, and on fairly good grounds (Marbach, 1968; Daniel, 1974a). More generally, the second, even if not the first, response to becoming unemployed is to set out to look for work (the first response, as we mentioned earlier, is quite often to have a 'break', to take a holiday, not least 'to think things over', p. 52). People certainly *see* themselves as seeking work on first becoming unemployed, and almost certainly do so; the evidence for this can be found not only in the relatively few accounts which actually cover the early days of being unemployed, but also in the case studies of the longer-term unemployed, reminiscing about their early days (Bakke, 1933; Beales and Lambert, 1934; Wedderburn, 1964; Gould and Kenyon, 1972; Marsden and Duff, 1975; Briar, 1977; Swinburn, 1981). It is clear from these accounts and reminiscences that initially the unemployed individual sees himself as making an effort: going to agencies, following up personal contacts, making telephone calls (since the fifties; we do not recall references to the telephone in the thirties), writing letters, trudging the streets, attending interviews, and so on. Gradually, however, when all this effort continues to be fruitless, he comes to see it as merely 'wasted effort', as just one more of the ways in which he has come to waste his time – which then merges into his general sense that his whole life is a waste (Harrison, 1976).

A very important unknown in all this is the transition from seeing oneself as an 'unemployed X' to seeing oneself as a 'one-time X'. Quite simply, how long can an individual continue to see himself *not* doing what has been his job, and still regard himself as someone who does that job? The issue is important because it is directly relevant to counselling the unemployed, and perhaps especially to the timing, as well as nature, of retraining. For some people the transition may be easy, even welcome; others may never make it at all. Such information as we have, and it is very little, relates almost exclusively to unemployed managers and professional people, and goes scarcely beyond recording that many did indeed eventually change careers and status, sometimes quite radically (Dyer, 1973; Briar, 1977): of the process, of the conflicts and the factors which finally resolved them, we know next to nothing. Furthermore, although the potential problem of such a transition may be at its most obvious in the case of clearly defined skills and professions, it might be a serious mistake to under-estimate it as also a problem for the semi-skilled and unskilled: an individual may feel attracted to an industry, even though his role within it is highly transferable; a porter at a steel-works might well not fancy being a doorman at a cosmetics firm.

It would also be a mistake to approach this problem as if it were primarily a function of personality, for example of individual differences in rigidity. The critical factor must be the criteria for labelling, and particularly for self-labelling, and these are affected by social norms and personal experience, as well as by any relatively innate personality traits. On judgement, an actor, for example, can probably remain unemployed and still remain 'an actor' to himself and others for much longer than a postman would remain 'a postman', a bank clerk 'a bank clerk', a university teacher 'a don'. The criteria which distinguish 'unemployed' from 'one-time' are to a considerable extent a matter of conventional and personal latitudes of acceptance (Sherif and Hovland, 1961): long and repeated periods of unemployment are more acceptable in relation to (and by) actors, than in relation to (and by) bank clerks and university teachers. However, these conventions and personal expectations largely reflect the relative probabilities of real life at a particular period of history; inasmuch as they do so, shifts in patterns of employment will in time induce shifts in related latitudes of acceptance. This is a difficult area for research. To disclose and trace shifts in latitudes of acceptance requires research which is extended over time, not merely longitudinally at the level of the individual, but even more so replicatively, over much longer periods, at the societal level: this is profoundly different from the 'one-off' approach which so predominates in psychological enquiry (Kelvin, 1984). It is, however, the only way in which to tackle the crucial question of how long one can continue *not* to do something and still regard doing it as an integral part of one's identity: and this is not only important for the psychological analysis of the effects of unemployment, but also for the general analysis of the nature of the self-concept.

So far we have considered how the unemployed individual looks on his or her behaviour. There is another area of self-observation: observation of simply how one looks. Although the literature is quite rich in references to appearance, these are scarcely ever more than asides: they are points noted in passing rather than explored – the outstanding exception is once again *Marienthal* (Jahoda *et al.*, 1933/72). In effect the bulk of psychological research on unemployment has been concerned with what may broadly be called 'states of mind', that is with the thoughts, feelings, and overall patterns of behaviour of the unemployed: it has almost wholly ignored 'conditions of the body'. There have, of course, been numerous studies of the medical concomitants of unemployment, but these are at other levels of discourse: Kasl and his group, for instance, were principally interested in basic physiological indices, attendance records, symptom check-lists (Kasl *et al.*, 1975); Brenner's studies, much disputed, dealt with the epidemiology of morbidity (e.g. Brenner, 1976); and, alternatively on the medical side, reports on the psychiatric condition of the unemployed have again, and quite properly, concentrated on 'states of mind', and broad patterns of behaviour (e.g. Fagin, 1980).

Our point is different. There is clear evidence in the literature, in autobiographies and case studies, from the seventies as well as the thirties, that the unemployed are affected by their own appearance. Their appearance has also often been recorded by researchers, but more to move our pity than to extend our understanding. Yet, and not least to give pity a practical dimension, there are problems here which need to be understood: there is need for research, at a psychological level of analysis, into the effects of unemployment on the *body-image*, just as there has been (and indeed as part of) research into its effects on the *self-concept*. Though the existing evidence is diffuse and mostly very bitty, we can identify at least a few of the major issues (Bakke, 1933; Pilgrim Trust, 1938; Hill, 1978).

There are two aspects of personal appearance: there is the appearance of the individual, literally as a *body*; and there is the appearance of his or her *clothes*: the two combine, with important practical consequences. Typically, the unemployed individual is recorded as looking drawn and gaunt. This may be a stereotype, to the point of being read into an individual's appearance, both by himself and by others. Even so, references to looking drawn, gaunt, or words to that effect, feature too consistently in writing about the unemployed to be mere imagination. We cannot tell how soon this gauntness sets in on becoming unemployed, and it is seldom mentioned in relation to school leavers or the young unemployed. It is, however, regularly referred to, even if only in passing, in connection with adults, and especially in connection with unemployed heads of households. One consequence is that wives often opt to go short on food themselves in order to ensure the fitness of their husbands – though both man as well as wife would cut their own food to provide 'properly' for their children. Particularly good, though very different, kinds of accounts of this pattern, are in Jahoda *et al.* (1933/72) and the Pilgrim Trust (1938) for the thirties, and in Marsden and Duff (1975) for the seventies. One area of research, therefore, is physical appearance as a source of anxiety, and the consequences of this for the whole house-hold.

In most cases *some* of the change of appearance will be due to a decline in the quality and quantity of food. Within this, granted that quality of food is likely to suffer through lack of money, it might be worth exploring whether there is a drop in quantity through lack of appetite because of depression, or on other psychological grounds, rather than on purely financial ones. To any change through loss of weight have to be added changes in posture and general loss of muscular tone, perhaps especially among men whose jobs had been demanding physically. Evidence for changes in posture and tone can be found in the early observations of slowed gait in *Marienthal*; in references to loafing, slouching, staying in bed (Bakke, 1933; Pilgrim Trust, 1938; Hill, 1978): falling off of timing and perhaps co-ordination is suggested by the use of pacemakers when an unemployed man returns to work (Bakke, 1933; also implicit in the concept of rehabilitation programmes, e.g. Hartlage and Johnson, 1971; Campling, 1978): it is implied in the generally avowed aims of rehabili-tation programmes to get the individual physically as well as psychologi-cally 'fit' for work.

Individuals vary in the extent to which they are aware of these often subtle changes of posture and gait. Some awareness is evident in accounts of 'typical' days, which are essentially self-descriptive state-ments; it is implied by the deliberate self-conscious steps taken by some unemployed to keep up appearances (Pilgrim Trust, 1938; Briar, 1977): and there is also evidence for the unemployeds' awareness of their physical condition from the very different context of research on the 'dis-couraged worker'. This last is a more complex matter, but it is relevant because of its practical implications. As we mentioned earlier, one feature of the 'discouraged worker' phenomenon is that the threshold for regarding oneself as 'unfit' is considerably lower in areas of high unem-ployment than in areas where unemployment is low (Daniel, 1974a). This indicates a fairly subtle integration of the perception of one's situ-ation with perception of one's physical condition. It also suggests that the unemployed individual in an area of high unemployment is in danger of being caught in a self-defeating downward spiral of self-labelling: the more frequently he finds himself disadvantaged competi-tively, the more easily he may see himself disabled personally.

Awareness of one's bodily condition (and of changes which may have occurred in it) interacts with awareness of the shabbiness of one's clothes (e.g. Pilgrim Trust, 1938; Marsden and Duff, 1975). Clothes wear out, of course, and the wearing out of shoes in particular seems to have been a very troublesome problem for the unemployed (Jahoda *et al.*, 1933/72). Sampling *The Times* over the period of the depression – which is salutary on several grounds – there are regular reports on the collection of boots and shoes for the unemployed; this was clearly a well-organised scheme of voluntary aid, presumably in answer to a very special and important need. But clothes do not wear out overnight. As we pointed out earlier, someone who had been in regular work would presumably enter unemployment with a stock of 'reasonable' attire which, in theory, should remain acceptable for some time. What may happen fairly quickly, however, is that loss of weight, and a slackening of gait, and especially of posture, make clothes 'hang' on one, too big, too loose – which may make them look much shabbier than in themselves they are. That is conjecture: the incontrovertible fact is that after a while, which may be quite short, most unemployed people become aware of changes in their appearance, changes which they see as reflecting and manifesting their depressed condition.

There remains one last and general point. Unemployment displaces the individual from a variety of settings in which he had previously felt himself to be embedded: that dislocation, and the need to reorient himself, would alone have been sufficient to increase his awareness of himself. In addition, one of the main problems of the unemployed individual is that he has so much time, and usually so few external demands on it. Almost inevitably, therefore, he is drawn into observing himself and his situation – much more so than he would have cause, need, or time to do if he were in work. Thus the unemployed individual is not only aware of being different from his fellows, he becomes even more different from them in being so aware of himself: and much of what he is aware of he dislikes, not only in his situation but also in himself. There is generally little to comfort him when he looks beyond himself at how he is seen by others.

# 6 The unemployed individual as seen by others

One of the core psychological assumptions about the self, certainly since William James (1890), is that the concept which an individual has of himself is profoundly influenced by the way in which he is seen and treated by others. As it might be told by the unemployed individual himself, it is the ways in which he *perceives* himself to be seen as 'unemployed'. From an objective standpoint, however, it is essential to establish how he is in fact seen by others, if only to assess whether his beliefs concerning their views are valid. An adequate account of the social psychological effects of unemployment must therefore encompass the reactions of others to the unemployed. This may seem obvious: the sad fact is that, in the case of the unemployed, assumptions about the importance of others has scarcely ever given rise to research amongst them. Psychological work on unemployment has so concentrated on the unemployed individual himself that it has virtually ignored the partners to his situation: with only very few exceptions it has treated them as no more than Rosencrantz and Guildenstern to his Hamlet.

The 'others' in the life of an individual could, in theory, be placed in a matrix of infinitesimal differences in terms of the extent and nature of their contact with him. In practice they are much more sensibly, and quite validly, grouped into a small number of broadly defined categories, which are functionally sufficiently different to make it desirable to distinguish between them. In the case of the unemployed there appear to be five such categories: the family; friends; social security and related agencies; employers; and 'the public' or 'society'. Only on one of these, the family, is there some evidence of the kind to which psychologists are accustomed, and there is little of that. There is nothing on the reactions of friends – except as reported by the unemployed themselves, which is another matter, to which we shall return. By narrowly empirical scientific criteria there is also almost no evidence on the reactions of the staffs of agencies, or of employers, or of 'the public'. For these, however, there is a variety of documentary and archival material, some of which may reasonably be taken to reflect attitudes and behaviour towards the unemployed – and may at least suggest issues for future empirical research. Here we can of course only point to the existence of this *kind* of material, and to its potential social psychological relevance, if only it were more fully explored.

## The family

There are four main sources of information on family reactions to the unemployed: *Marienthal* (Jahoda *et al.*, 1933/72), and *The Unemployed Man and His Family* (Komarovsky, 1940) from the thirties; *Workless* (Marsden and Duff, 1975), and *The Effect of Unemployment on Workers and their Families* (Briar, 1977). We know of other work in progress, or not yet published in full (e.g. Fagin, 1980), but at the time of writing these four still seem to be the only studies which deliberately included some examination of the family life of the unemployed. To these must, however, be added the countless passing references to the reactions of wives, children, and other relatives in other research, and evidence which implies their reactions. One example of such a glimpse is a finding which we mentioned a few pages ago: in some communities a wife will not hold a job while her man is unemployed (Sinfield, 1981); she sees him as already reduced in status and hurt in self-respect, and as potentially further undermined if she were to succeed where he was currently failing. Another example is the young working son (or daughter) who finds a job with his firm for his middle-aged unemployed father (Ohashi, 1975 a, b; Sinfield, 1981). This is not only evidence of filial concern, but also of a partial, however slight, reversal of traditional roles: though 'following in father's footsteps' may be rare in fact, the saying reflects an ingrained assumption that it is the father who creates opportunities for his son, not the son for his father. In different ways, both these examples are instances of a probably quite general consequence of unemployment, at least for husbands, fathers, 'heads of households': unemployment leads to a change in the perceived direction of dependence.

There is therefore a modicum of evidence on how the unemployed are seen by members of their families, but its sources are diffuse, and its nature is often fragmentary. Even the four richest studies form a very heterogeneous group. If we assume that family relationships are significantly influenced by culture, then he have: Marienthal, an Austrian village, predominantly working class, whose family life will, presumably, have been largely shaped by Roman Catholicism; we have Komarovsky's sample, drawn from an East Coast American city, large, industrial, close to New York, its members specifically selected as being Protestant, skilled or white-collared by occupation, and white; Marsden and Duff's people were British, and ranged from the unskilled through semi-skilled to skilled men with some managerial experience; Briar's work takes us back to the United States, but this time to the northern end of the West Coast (Puget Sound, Wa.), with a sample which was roughly half non-professional and young, and half professional and middle-aged. Between them, these four studies cover interesting and perhaps important variations in culture and sub-culture; any theme which is common to them all may, therefore, reflect underlying processes which are indeed basic and very general. An element of caution would, however, be advisable. Each of these four is the sole representative of its kind: its wider validity within its own culture remains to be established. This is not just pedantry. Consider, for example, the case of Marienthal: the dominant culture of Austria in the thirties was rooted in the Catholic church; the church does not feature in the account of Marienthal, and we learn from the introduction that Marienthal did not have a church of its own: on judgement, this makes Marienthal somewhat unusual for its time and place generally; and, more particularly, it may help to explain the utter dependence of the people of Marienthal on its one factory, as the focus of their social as well as of their economic lives. These four studies are too thinly spread to provide a basis for really confident gener-alisation. As for the rest of the evidence, it is mostly piecemeal and cir-cumstantial. At the end one is therefore left with no more than *impressions*.

With that important proviso, the unemployed man around the house tends to be seen as inclined to withdraw into himself, and as irritable: his turning in on himself worries other members of the household, his irrita-bility makes him irritating in his turn. Where his 'authority' rested on his role as a provider, that authority, or respect, is often much reduced – oc-casionally but only occasionally – to the level of contempt (Komarovsky, 1940, has particularly vivid cases of this). Partly related to this, he is often (and probably correctly) seen to have lost his self-confidence: even to supportive wives and older children he looks less positive, less the man he was – which is *not*, please note, the same as seeming less of a 'man', though some may feel that too. Perhaps most important of all, he seems somehow less *physically*: he may in fact, of course, have lost some weight (Pilgrim Trust, 1938); more subtly, but probably more significantly, there is that loss of tone in posture and gait on which we have remarked earlier; to those who know him, therefore, he may well seem to have shrunk. There is, presumably, some interaction between psychological withdrawal and physical shrinking, not only as this may actually happen to the unemployed individual, but also as it appears to be happening to him when he is observed by others. How much of this is imagined and how much real, and which is a cue for what, is a question for future research.

His family, then, sees the unemployed individual as having 'a problem', and to that extent he is a problem to them – as a *person*, and not simply because he is, for example, failing in his economic role. Whether he is then treated as someone who needs gentling or kicking, or some mixture of both, is quite another matter. Much, it seems, depends on the individual's basic standing with his family: unemployment rarely transforms relationships, but rather polarises prior patterns, towards greater supportiveness or more precipitate collapse (Komarovsky, 1940; Fagin, 1980; see also pp. 59–61, above).

The evidence so far allows three *tentative* generalisations:

1   Unemployment polarises rather than transforms basic patterns of family relationships. The *quality* of the particular changes wrought by unemployment will be mainly determined by the nature of relationships before it.
2   Within this, unemployment may change both the actual and perceived direction of dependencies within the family. (This change in who depends emotionally on whom must not be confused with the not infrequent, practical, redistribution of domestic chores; the two may be connected, but not necessarily).
3   The family may see the unemployed man as 'less-than-the-man-he-was', sympathetically or disdainfully, depending on earlier relations.

Like all generalisations, these are no more than initial hypotheses: but at least they are a beginning.

### Friends

As regards friends, we unfortunately do not even begin to know how the unemployed individual is *actually* seen by his friends: and it would make negligible difference to this overall assessment if we were to distinguish between those of his friends who were employed, and those who were out of work themselves. One can certainly find reports and comments on the behaviour of friends in case-studies of the unemployed, occasionally confirmed and enlarged upon by the comments of wives, and even children (see especially Komarovsky, 1940; Marsden and Duff, 1975; Briar, 1977; Swinburn, 1981). This material, however, is primarily evidence of how the unemployed (and their families) *perceive* their friends, and how they perceive themselves to be seen, which is a very different standpoint. Of the friends as such, that is of individuals studied in their role of 'friend', we know nothing. There simply does not seem to have been any research on the effects of unemployment on friendships, and especially on prior friendships, from the perspective of the unemployed's friends.

It has to be said that it may well be almost impossible to research this issue. To work outwards, from the unemployed individual to his circle of friends, might often seem intolerably intrusive to him, and could be deeply embarrassing to his friends: it is potentially too disruptive to relationships to be morally and therefore ethically acceptable. It might seem easier, and more acceptable, to move inwards – in the sense of, say, talking to employed people who have unemployed friends. The great limitation of this approach is that one would almost certainly encounter only the more active, positive relationships, rather than those which had become tentative, or had virtually, or wholly, collapsed. Yet the phenomenon which distresses and demoralises the unemployed is precisely the once-open relationship which, as they see it, has become guarded; the close contact who has become distant; the friendships that seem to have ended.

It is therefore inherently very difficult to explore the effects of unemployment on friendship from the position of the friend – at least in a way which is both sensitive to the situation and scientifically valid: and we must also recognise that until we solve this problem, the social psychological analysis of the effects of unemployment on friendship will remain inadequately one-sided. This is serious. For example, while the unemployed quite often talk of former friends who have withdrawn, we also know that the unemployed themselves often withdraw from social life, if only because they cannot afford it. Furthermore, there are ecological as well as economic factors: where a relationship, even a close relationship, was significantly based on work and the work-place, unemployment may significantly reduce the probability of encounter (Festinger *et al.*, 1950); effort would have to be made to remain in touch, only to lead to the discovery that there is little left in common, little left to talk about. Who therefore withdraws from whom, to what extent, and why? To account for the social psychological consequences of unemployment requires information on the actual social psychological circumstances of the unemployed, as well as on their own perception of these: our ignorance of the perspective of friends is therefore a profound weakness; it will be very difficult to overcome.

## Agencies

Compared with the almost complete absence of information on how the unemployed individual is seen by his friends, there is at least a little evidence on how he is perceived by the agencies which deal with his problems and welfare. The evidence is limited and indirect. It is limited in that it relates only to the main statutory and public agencies, for example the Benefit Offices: we have not found any studies on what we would call 'voluntary' agencies, such as for example the Child Poverty Action Group. It is indirect in that it consists of only scattered bits of information, from a variety of sources, which *imply* attitudes to the unemployed: it is not based on, say, systematic attitude surveys among agency staffs. Nevertheless, for all its limitations, there is some intrinsic interest in the little we have; and it might just be of some practical use.

Two items of evidence we have mentioned already, in connection with the search for work (pp. 26–41). First, when the Job Centres have knowledge of vacancies, they put forward the recently unemployed, rather than those who have been unemployed for several months. There are good pragmatic grounds for this: employers seem to be suspicious of the longer-term unemployed; such a person is therefore not very likely to get the job; the Job Centre's job is to get people jobs; no one benefits if the Centre tries to place the less acceptable before the more acceptable. In effect the career of many a 'discouraged worker' will probably have begun by his image within the agency as a discouraging prospect – which grows steadily as the period of his unemployment lengthens.

Secondly, we remarked earlier that quite especial efforts are sometimes made to find jobs for the truly long-term unemployed, who have been through rehabilitation and training centres (Campling, 1978: p. 32). Obviously the prime function and sole justification of a centre, and of those who run it, is to make the trainees fit for work; and to that extent the centres have a vested interest in the success of their products. There is another factor in the situation, however: a training centre is the one agency with whose staff the unemployed individual can form a *working* relationship. Out of this then grows a kind of 'protective' attitude on the part of staff, a twentieth-century, bureaucratic version of 'patronage', which sometimes helps the trainee to appointments which he would have had very little hope indeed of obtaining otherwise. We would stress the 'sometimes': not all trainees are likely to be equally favoured; the same working relationship which can gain one trainee the confidence of staff can confirm the worst suspicions in the case of another.

It would be very useful to know how subtly the staffs of training centres discriminate between their trainees, and particularly on what grounds. We do not know of any research specifically concerned with this issue. The nearest we have is research on *programmes* for training the unemployed, and this has to be treated very circumspectly. The programmes on which there is published evidence were predominantly American, and designed for the long-term, hard-core unemployed, sometimes more chastely called 'the hard to employ'. These programmes cannot be regarded as similar to the various British schemes set up in response to the recent sharp rise in unemployment among the essentially 'normal' working population. However, one item of evidence from these studies is of general relevance, if only because it discloses something so obvious that it is usually ignored: the great majority of programmes, and therefore presumably of those who run them, seem to be based on the assumption that *attitudes cause behaviour*. As a consequence, one of the most important tasks conceived for a programme has been to change the individual's attitude – towards work, towards himself or herself, towards discipline and authority, and so on (e.g. O'Leary, 1972; Beatty, 1975; Beatty and Beatty, 1975; Salipante and Goodman, 1976; Briar, 1977; Campling, 1978). Given a successful change of attitude, the assumption is that change of behaviour will follow, and will lead to success in finding and retaining a job. This is, of course, the traditional concept of 'attitudes', which is held by the layman as 'naive psychologist' (Heider, 1958), in which the direction of causality is perceived as running from attitudes to behaviour. It ignores the long line of theory and evidence which shows that the direction of causality is often *from* behaviour *to* attitudes. (One could arguably trace this back to the James–Lange theory of emotion, 1890s; and certainly from, say, Gordon Allport's 'functional autonomy of motives' (1937), through Festinger's dissonance theory (1957), to self-perception theory (Bem, 1967, 1972).) This 'naive' approach of programmes has indeed been repeatedly questioned at an academic level. To take just one simple but very practical example: Salipante and Goodman (1976) have shown that training on attitudes to work is, if anything, *negatively* related to holding on to a job; what matters is being given the relevant skills, which enable one to 'behave' appropriately in the work situation, simply through being able to get on with the job. More generally, the attitudes of any one unemployed individual are in any case only one part of the total problem: successful integration into a job depends crucially on the behaviour and attitudes (in *that* order) of fellow workers, supervisors, management and, often, the individual's sub-culture outside work (Feldman, 1973a,b; Beatty, 1974; perhaps especially Triandis *et al.*, 1975; and Goodman and Salipante, 1976).

It is one thing for an ordinary layman to be a 'naive psychologist', quite another for an official to be so. If an ordinary layman is psychologically naive, and if the inadequacies of that naivety lead him to wrong decisions, the consequences of his mistakes are visited on himself at least as much as on others, and probably much more so. When an official is naive, say the manager of a Benefit Office, the consequences of wrong decisions affect first and foremost those who depend on him, and only secondarily, and indirectly (and often not at all) himself. Considered simply as a basic learning situation, feedback and reinforcement, and therefore the chance of learning from mistakes, are much more direct in the case of the layman than of even the best-intentioned but naive official. From our standpoint, however, the important implications are at that very subtle level of the perception of others, the level of attribution of responsibilities and causes. In arriving at some of their most basic decisions, the staff at Benefit Offices, are, for instance, explicitly charged with assessing for each individual the extent to which he is himself responsible for his situation – to assess, for example, whether he is genuinely seeking work; and to withhold benefit if he is not. The naive approach, which assigns causal priority to attitudes, leads to the belief that an individual's unemployment, stems from his attitudes; it ignores the distinct possibility that behaviour and attitudes may stem *from* his unemployment. The irony is that another person's attitudes are, of course, not directly observable as such; they can only be *inferred* by observers precisely from his behaviour. Given this, the range of an individual's behaviour which is 'visible' to the staff of an agency is usually no more than a small and circumscribed sub-routine of his total behaviour repertoire – and moreover one which is highly contingent to the setting of the agency. The evidence from which agency staff can infer attitudes is therefore normally very limited, the one possible exception being the evidence from training centres.

There is an important basic issue here, which is common to all relationships between individuals and agencies, and which is perhaps best brought out by comparing the way in which an individual is perceived by his family with the way in which he is seen by an agency. Within the family, and among friends, the individual is seen first and foremost as a whole *person*, and only secondly in some specific role, such as 'breadwinner', one of the darts team, and so on. Perceived as a person, he fills many roles, bringing to each of these a touch of his particular uniqueness (Emmerich, 1961; Kelvin, 1970). From the standpoint of an agency, however, he is seen first and foremost in his *role* as an 'unemployed', as a 'claimant', as a 'client'. Since various agencies differ in their aims and functions, the finer details of his role will also differ from agency to agency: as claimant at the Benefit Office; as job-hunter at the Job Centre; as client with, say, the Family Welfare Association. The details may vary, but the basic social psychological situation is nevertheless always that of a *role relationship*, not of a *personal relationship*. This is so by definition, but it is reasonable to assume that this definition is in fact valid in the vast majority of cases. Some agencies do seek to establish something closer to a personal relationship with the individual as a whole; and occasionally, in a small agency, something approaching personal relationships may indeed be achieved. Occasionally, also, an individual case-worker may form a truly personal relationship with one of his or her clients. In the nature of the situation, however, this cannot happen very often. Personal relationships take time to develop and time to maintain: caseworkers are notoriously overloaded with work; in practice, therefore, the *raison d'être* of their relationships with the vast majority of their cases will remain the position of the unemployed in his *role* of claimant or client. It follows that attitudes towards a particular unemployed individual will be significantly, even if not wholly, determined by his or her *conformity* to the expectations associated with that role. These expectations are, of course, essentially those of a *stereotype*, the stereotype of 'The Unemployed', 'The Claimant', 'The Client', and so on – as conceptualised by those working in a particular agency and affected by its particular terms and frames of reference.

It would not be difficult to research the stereotypes of 'The Unemployed', and attitudes and behaviour towards them, amongst the staffs of agencies. There would be none of the technical and ethical problems which are inescapable in research among an unemployed individual's friends. The chances are that some agencies have indeed carried out such research amongst their staffs, but, if so, the findings seem to have remained for internal consumption only. This is neither surprising nor unreasonable. Unfortunately it means that we have no direct evidence on how the unemployed are perceived by agency staffs, but there are two studies which indirectly provide several relevant clues.

The first study is American, Lipsky's *Street Corner Bureaucracy* (1981). The title refers nicely and neatly to the actual goings-on, at *local* level, in the administration of would-be 'central' welfare policies. Patterns of street-corner bureaucracy may in turn be taken as symptomatic of some of the most basic attitudes of staff, whether at a particular street corner or, as it were, at the sharp end generally. Lipsky suggests, for example, that day-to-day arrangements, such as for interviewing, reflect a fundamental assumption that the time of officials is more significant and valuable than that of claimants or clients.

Though in matters of unemployment and social security the import (and export) of ideas has to be handled with a certain caution, the term and concept of 'street-corner bureaucracy' deserves dissemination: it articulates the essence of that very important phenomenon, the discrepancy between central policies and their local implementation. The phenomenon is almost certainly quite as prevalent in the United Kingdom as elsewhere – which brings us to our second study. This was conceptually similar to Lipsky's, and was undertaken by Anthony Laurance of the Department of Health and Social Security. We have not ourselves seen this report: it appears to have been 'internal' and 'confidential'. It does, however, seem to have been 'leaked' (*not* by Mr Laurance himself), and articles based on it have appeared in *New Society* (Moore, 1980) and elsewhere (Douglas, 1980). It is a report of, in effect, six months of participant observation in an inner-city Benefit Office. It is clear from the account of this (as reported in secondary sources), that the development of street-corner bureaucracy is inevitable, and with it the discrepancies between the policies at headquarters (*sic*) and their execution in the field. For example, central policy is to advise and help claimants, and not only to document cases and arrange benefit. Concern for the individual is, unfortunately, very labour-intensive. In practice, at the front line where it matters, the office was seriously understaffed: it also had a high turn-over of staff; its business, if it were to get done at all, had to be done briskly – often, as the claimant would experience it, brusquely. Shortages of staff at local offices would therefore be quite sufficient on their own to undermine those aspects of central policy whose aim was care at the level of the individual. The situation was made much worse by the need of local offices to demonstrate their efficiency to regional and central management. This is perfectly proper and, in theory, it would indeed be a safeguard for claimants. That, too, goes awry however: for performance is assessed primarily in terms of quantitative output, for example in terms of callers handled, numbers interviewed:

this reliance on statistics distorts the offices' work and perspective. Too much importance is attached to work which can be measured, however low in priority, however irrelevant . . .                                                  (Moore, 1980, p. 69)

The academic reader has no grounds to feel superior: the same mentality is constantly manifest in appointments and promotions at universities, and for quite the same reason. *Quantities*, whether of clients processed or of publications, are readily demonstrated: sets of quantities can be ordered and compared without ambiguity, argument or fear of refutation, and even in total ignorance of what it is they quantify. Qualities, on the other hand, can only be evaluated; their evaluation rests on informed personal judgement, which is open to dispute and therefore risky: and so the modern administrator, whether bureaucratic or academic, has found a new meaning for 'safety in numbers'. From the standpoint of staff, quality of work will, of course, receive much lip-service; but fundamentally it will go unnoticed, and it may indeed be positively counter-productive: for the time taken by care over quality is at the expense of what, quite literally, counts – namely productivity measured in numbers. In the particular case of local Benefit Offices, shortages of staff combine with the ethos of quantification to reduce the claimant into one of so-and-so-many for processing. There is neither the time nor the incentive to deal with him as an individual. The conditions under which street-corner bureaucracy operates make it inevitable that it operates in terms of stereotype concepts of claimants.

Important elements of the stereotype will follow simply and directly from the nature of the officer–claimant relationships. Role relationships give rise to a stereotype or, perhaps better, to a 'model' of the ideal role occupant. Fom the position of the often hard-pressed official, then, the model claimant is defined in terms of ease of processing: punctual for interviews: efficient in providing documentary evidence concerning himself and his claim; sufficiently well informed to be helpful, but not well enough informed to pursue points of detail; co-operative and appreciative of the officer – and so on. Conversely, the role relationship also defines the stereotype of the 'awkward': awkward administratively in unreliability for interviews and inability to provide essential documents; full of having been told of his entitlements; and perhaps especially awkward in wanting to be treated as a unique individual with unique *personal* problems, rather than in his *role* within an inevitably bureaucratic system. The models may seldom be as openly articulated as we have here made them, but their existence can be inferred quite unequivocally from a variety of evidence (e.g. Stevenson, 1973; Weightman, 1978; Coussins, 1980; Moore, 1980; Lipsky, 1981).

The models of the 'good' and the 'awkward' claimant are, of course, simply models of two very basic, general types. Superimposed on these are the particular features of particular classes of claimant, such as pensioners, or single parents, or, as in our case, the unemployed. The most direct evidence we have on this is again from the study by Laurance, which covered only one Benefit Office, and of which we know only from secondary sources. On its own this is scarcely the basis for confident generalisations. Neither, however, is it wholly to be discounted: it is consistent with, and to that extent confirmed by, indirect evidence from other sources (e.g. Gould and Kenyon, 1972; Marsden and Duff, 1975; and, from a more 'administrative' orientation, again Stevenson, 1973; Sinfield, 1981).

We need not make any assumptions about any personal biases of Benefit Office staff: we need to consider only their situation, and the consequences which are bound to flow from it. The spirit of policy, as of law, would insist that the function of Benefit Office staff is to help the unemployed claimant and to encourage him to continue to look for work. This last, the encouragement to find work, is ostensibly a particularly important function of Unemployment Review Officers: their task 'in the interest both of claimants and public accountability' is to keep all claimants 'under review' on their efforts to find work (Report of the Supplementary Benefit Commission, 1979, p. 50; quoted Sinfield, 1981, p. 115). In practice the overriding concern has been with only one side of the problem, public accountability. Even that one-sided approach could be highly productive. Public accountability as a process and discipline is itself highly desirable, if it leads to money well spent; the fact, however, is that 'public accountability' has come to stand simply for 'saving money', rather than for ensuring its most effective use. The failure is intellectual even more than moral, and little is therefore gained by moral or political indignation. We are back at the problem of quantitative assessment versus qualitative evaluation. Money is a *quantity*, the expenditure and savings of which can be calculated very precisely: much of what it buys, perhaps most of it, and of what is foregone through inability to buy, is significant for its *qualitative* elements. At an administrative level, expenditure and savings show up in the books, the quality of service and welfare, or of the hardship which flow from lack of them, do not. It is not surprising, therefore, that the ability to show 'savings' has become a major criterion for assessing the effectiveness of Benefit Offices, and a major preoccupation of their staffs (Moore, 1980; Sinfield, 1981, partly based on Moore).

One very visible means of saving is, of course, on staff itself, which leads to shortages of staff: this, and its consequences, we have discussed already. The other principal source of savings is on benefit paid out – or rather, not paid out. The unemployed are especially vulnerable in this respect. A pensioner, for example, is a pensioner; and nothing an official might do can alter that fact. Similarly, single parents are single parents, and Benefit Offices staff do not have the power to arrange marriages. In the case of pensioners and single parents, therefore, savings can only be achieved on points of detail, on the amount of benefit allocated. The discretionary powers of local officers may be considerable, but once a pensioner or a single parent has been accepted as such, the only factor which can change those statuses is time. In the case of the unemployed, status is in theory eminently reversible, and at any moment, simply by the claimant finding work: very considerable 'savings' can therefore be achieved by unemployed claimants returning to work. The Unemployment Review Officer is therefore under considerable pressure himself to 'encourage' return to work.

The preoccupation with savings combines with the obsession with the ferreting out and hounding down of 'welfare scroungers'. The evidence of scrounger-hounding is beyond dispute, and shows this to be so disproportionate that it is important to recognise it as an obsession – so that it be replaced by a more rational and therefore more effective response. We shall return to this when we consider 'public opinion' and the unemployed. In the present context the crucial fact is that the task of ferreting out has been put squarely on the staff of Benefit Offices: they have to assess not only levels of need and benefit; when they are dealing with an unemployed it is an integral part of their duties to check whether the claimant is genuinely unemployed, and seeking work – rather than scrounging by living off the state, with occasional undeclared earnings on the side.

It would be absurd to deny that there are scroungers: all social systems have members who exploit them, and the system has in its own interest to reduce these to a minimum. The sad thing is, as Laurance's study shows, that the duty to identify scroungers, combined with the general incentive to make savings, distorts the operations of Benefit Office staff, and inevitably affects their attitudes. They are bound, in a very real sense duty bound, to be suspicious: and the

relatively rare instances which confirm the need for vigilance are all the more reinforcing for being intermittent:

> 'It was also the more outrageous cases of fraud or abuse that had become the common gossip of the office ... Because there was a *possibility* of fraud in so many cases, an air of suspicion commonly underlay interviews and was hard to conceal. Questioning a claimant with one eye on his welfare needs, and the other on the possibility of fraud, was an impossibly schizophrenic role. And with some of the staff the suspicious eye became much the sharper of the two.'
>
> (Laurance, quoted Moore, 1980, p. 69. Our italics)

The situation of Benefit Office staff is deeply ambiguous. The basic language of benefit both reveals and helps to maintain the underlying ambiguity. The word 'claim' has two connotations: there is 'claim' in the sense of 'due', 'right', 'title to', or 'to demand'; and there is claim in the sense of 'allegation' or 'to allege', with quite strong implications of possible falsehood: claiming one's bride after the wedding-breakfast and claiming to be sober at the time are not the same kind of claim. There is also the important distinction between the concept of a 'claimant' and the concept of a 'client' (see particularly Stevenson, 1973). We shall have more to say on the nature of the language of unemployment later: for the moment simply consider, for example, the underlying mismatch in communication if the dominant connotation of the word 'claim' is 'entitlement' to an unemployed individual, while to a Benefit Officer it is 'allegation-to-be-sustained'.

We began by arguing that the relationship between the unemployed individual and the staffs of agencies is for all practical purposes bound to be a role relationship, not a personal relationship. It is one of the well-established facts of social psychology (and organisational psychology) that the effectiveness of a role relationship is defined and perceived by the partners to it. Conversely, inadequate definition and perceived ambiguities are recognised sources of intra-role strain and inter-role conflict, and of consequent ineffectiveness, stress, and trouble (see Katz and Kahn, 1978, for an authoritative account and discussion from the standpoint of organisational psychology).

By these criteria, the situation of Benefit Office staff is singularly bad. In essence, local levels are left to resolve in their practice the ambivalence which central policy-makers proclaim by their principles. One aspect of central policy demands that the unemployed individual is advised and helped, which means handling him with sympathy and gaining his confidence; the other aspect requires that scroungers be identified and rooted out, which means treating him with suspicion: it is the local office which has to find how to gain an individual's confidence by treating him as suspect. The day-to-day problems which arise from this are no doubt partly reduced by the division of labour within offices, as, for example, between clerical officers at the counter and Unemployment Review Officers. Nevertheless, the ambivalence of central policy creates a situation at local levels which is deeply ambiguous: one of the principal ways of resolving such ambiguity is to assign much more significance to one of the competing options than to the other. This is what seems to be happening, and the option predominantly chosen appears to be the identification, prevention, and rooting out of fraud – that is suspicion.

The chances are (but we have no evidence for this) that the way in which any one actual unemployed individual is seen will be much influenced by the length of his unemployment. Someone only recently unemployed, and with a reasonably 'good' history of employment, is most unlikely to be regarded as suspect from the very start. Similarly there will be the 'old customers', whose record of failure to find work, or of inability to keep it, will be well known in the office, and who have thus transcended suspicion. The case most vulnerable to suspicion will often, and sadly, be the individual who is also most vulnerable psychologically in himself: the individual who doesn't know where he is going; whether he is an unemployed 'X' or a one-time 'X', whether he should change the kind of work he does; whether he should 'trade down', or even withdraw himself from the work-force – and so forth. In effect, the individual who perhaps is most in need of help is also the one who is most likely to be treated with suspicion: but this is conjecture.

We may seem to have given an excessive amount of attention to the way in which the unemployed individual is perceived by the staffs of agencies – especially since the very little evidence we have derives from only one public sector agency. Our justification is that this is a most important area for further social psychological research. The public sector agencies constitute the most substantial point of real, practical, contact between the unemployed individual and 'society'. In principle it is here that the attitudes of society are translated into action, and thereby significantly help to shape the attitudes of the unemployed individual to society. As we have seen, the present situation is a mess of ambiguities and ambivalences. Tempting though it might be, it would be intellectually as well as morally dishonest to attribute this mess solely, or even mainly, to those who make policy at the centre and those who execute it locally. The confusion permeates the whole of society; it has done so for centuries; and it is essential to the social psychological analysis of unemployment to recognise this. Before we turn to that very general phenomenon, however, we must briefly consider one other group which is very important to the unemployed – their potential employers.

## Employers

Employers enter the situation of the unemployed at two diametrically opposed points: at firing and at hiring. Except that, once again, the situation is not quite so simple. In talking and writing about 'the unemployed', especially at a time of recession, the natural tendency is to assume that the unemployed are for all practical purposes people who have been made redundant by new technologies and low levels of economic activity. The first fact, then, is that there are *three* main classes of reasons for which an unemployed individual may have left his last job: he may have left of his own accord; because of redundancy; and because he was dismissed (this applies, of course, only to people who have had work; school leavers and others in search of their first job constitute a special category and a special problem; see the Introduction). The second fact is that even as late as 1980/81 strictly the largest group of registered unemployed had left their last job of their own accord (37%), though the proportion of redundant was virtually identical (36%); only 14.5% had been dismissed (Daniel, 1981: the remainder is accounted for by a variety of more individual reasons). In Daniel's 1973 sample (which included women) 47% had left of their own accord, 28% had been made redundant, and 20% had been dismissed (Daniel, 1974a). The years 1973 and 1974 may seem 'another world'. To see all this in perspective, therefore, the important and influential study by Marsden and Duff, published in 1975, was based on fieldwork conducted in 1972 – and 43% of the respondents interviewed in Daniel's 1973/4 research had been unemployed for over twelve months, which therefore encompasses the period covered by Marsden and Duff.

There is another fact, as it were from the other end of the problems. We know, or can infer from archival and documentary evidence, that employers are reluctant to hire the unemployed (Beveridge, 1909/31; Daniel, 1974a; Hawkins, 1979; Sinfield, 1981). It is only reasonable to assume that their stance towards unemployed applicants will be at least partly influenced by their own experience of how workers come to leave or lose their jobs. From the employers' standpoint, then, almost all unemployment due to having left of one's own accord, and all due to dismissal, will be seen as essentially self-inflicted. Within this, leaving work of one's own accord was on grounds of general dissatisfaction, dissatisfaction with pay, rows with fellow workers: and grounds of dismissal, were, for example, faulty work, bad time-keeping, disputes with fellow workers, and bosses. In 1973, being dismissed or having left of one's own accord accounted for around two-thirds of Daniel's very careful sample; and these two classes still accounted for around one-half of his 1980 sample: and the most 'acceptable' grounds under both headings, illness or injury, may also contain elements of the self-inflicted, and would tend to undermine confidence in the physical fitness of an applicant (for fuller details, see Daniel, 1974a, tables VI: 3 and VI: 8; and Daniel, 1981, table III: 7).

Different industries have different patterns of employment and unemployment, for example in terms of their seasonality; the significance which an employer attaches to someone in his trade or business being unemployed will inevitably vary with this. Nevertheless, inasmuch as these *aggregate* figures reflect the experiences of employers in the *aggregate*, they contribute to explaining why it is that employers tend to be reluctant to hire the unemployed: why should an employer hire someone who, on a balance of probabilities, is quite likely to be one or more of incompetent, dissatisfied, unpunctual, quarrelsome with workmates, and so on? This last is, however, only conjecture: we do not know of any empirical research on employers' attitudes towards the generality of unemployed workers. There has been some research related to the employment problems of particular groups, for example the hard-core unemployed of ethnic minorities in the United States (e.g. Di Marco and Gustafson, 1975; Goodman and Salipante, 1976). We have not, however, encountered any study of the experiences of employers with the 'ordinary' unemployed, and how this affects their attitudes and policies towards them. Since ultimately the fate of the unemployed and much of the condition of the economy and of society depends on the *re*-employment of the unemployed, this means that we have no information on one of the most crucial aspects of the whole unemployment situation.

To illustrate the kinds of problem involved we shall confine ourselves to just two sets of issues. First, to what extent, if any, do employers distinguish between 'self-inflicted' unemployment, and redundancy? Since the first is primarily attributable to the individual, and the other primarily to economic conditions or technological change, one might predict that the redundant worker would fare better than those who had left their last job of their own accord, or who had been dismissed: on the other hand, 'redundant' may have come to be treated as a euphemism for 'dismissal', and thus have little special significance; or it might suggest out-dated skills, or association with failure, which might be counter-productive for finding work. That is at a conceptual level.

The second set of issues arises from the evidence that unemployment leads to a loss of tone in posture and gait (see pp. 73–6, above.) We speculated earlier that such loss of tone may become a non-verbal cue to other people of lack of interest, motivation, stamina, or a sense of defeat, and so on. In addition, the unemployed individual often feels shabby and, in due course, as resources run out, very likely does look shabby. How, then, does he look to potential employers? Clothes may not matter much in the case of unemployed manual workers, many of whom are interviewed and hired on the site; but their posture and gait may be very significant, as cues of fitness, drive, being 'on the ball': and clothes, as well as posture and gait, almost certainly matter whenever 'presence' matters, from opening doors to customers to negotiating multi-million dollar contracts. We know nothing about the unemployed in the hiring situation. What is it that so often seems to put him at a disadvantage, compared to an applicant currently at work? The fact that the unemployed is unemployed will, after all, mostly be known *before* he is interviewed. And conversely, what is it about the unemployed applicant who *does* succeed, despite the fact that the employer knows that he is unemployed?

Research on the perceptions of employers of the 'ordinary' unemployed would certainly be complex. Not only are there the differences in the employment patterns of different industries, there is also the basic difficulty of defining who is the 'employer'. The decision-making process and the decision-makers will certainly vary with the nature of the vacant job and the size of the firm. There may, therefore, be considerable problems in identifying the critical individuals, before one can even start on substantive issues – issues such as, say, the perceived costs to the decision-maker of an error of judgement, and the perceived riskiness of appointing someone who was unemployed. It is a difficult area of research, but one in which social psychology might make a particularly useful contribution. Though an individual's unemployment may often have been caused by strictly economic factors, it may even more often be unnecessarily delayed by strictly non-economic ones, that is by his own behaviour, and by his perceived status as a result of being unemployed. The unemployed and employers might well both gain if each saw how he looked to the other, why, and with what justification: and that is social psychological research *par excellence*.

### 'Society'/'public opinion'

One of the most central psychological phenomena of unemployment is the ambivalence of 'society' or 'public opinion' towards the unemployed. This is far from being merely of academic interest, because public opinion makes a direct impact on the unemployed, and in two ways. First, it defines the stereotype of 'The Unemployed': that stereotype greatly influences how a given individual, known as 'unemployed' is perceived and treated generally – 'generally', as distinct from how he is perceived and treated by his close family and friends, who know him as a person. Secondly, public opinion has a significant effect on how the unemployed are treated by 'society', as represented by the state: for the provision which the state makes for the unemployed, both in its extent and in the conditions under which it is available, is very largely determined by public opinion.

For our purposes, 'society', 'the attitudes of society', 'public opinion', will all refer to the attitudes and opinions attributed to 'people' – whether in so many words, as 'people generally', or as in 'the ordinary person', or 'the ordinary citizen', or 'they' – or whatever else the collective term might be, including 'society', 'community', and 'public opinion' itself. We cannot here explore what it may be that the notions 'public opinion' or 'attitudes of society' might denote, as it were, 'in nature'. Our concern is limited to the consequences of a much simpler and incontrovertible fact: people, as individual members of society, *believe* that there is some entity to which it is meaningful to refer as 'public opinion', or some connotatively identical term: that this public opinion 'demands', 'insists', 'ensures', 'condones', 'condemns', will or will not 'tolerate', and so on, whatever is the object of its attention: that *because* it is 'public opinion', it significantly influences behaviour in relation to that object; and that it thus helps to explain and justify that behaviour. So, for example, the unemployed individual feels stigmatised because he believes public opinion regards the unemployed as 'scroungers'; and the politician demands, in the name of public opinion, that scroungers be hounded down and eliminated.

The literature is curious: it is much influenced by myth and folk-lore; it is rich in assumptions, particularly in assumptions by one set of people, say the press or politicians, about the assumptions of others, such as 'ordinary people'; but anything which might be called substantive empirical *evidence* is virtually non-existent. As regards the United Kingdom, we know of only one piece of fieldwork which investigated public opinion concerning the unemployed in any detail, and even then as only one aspect of public opinion on Supplementary Benefit as a whole: the report of this study is not generally available, but may be obtained, on application, and after clearance, from the Central Office of Information (Schlackman Research Organisation Ltd, 1978). The scale of this research was small, its nature qualitative (twelve group discussions, thirty-two depth interviews), but, since it is the only relevant empirical work we have found, it seems justifiable to quote from its conclusions:

With the *exception* of the unemployed, there is a broad acceptance that the remaining groups [e.g. pensioners, single parent families] merit assistance and can maintain their standard of living at a level comparable to other people's. For the unemployed ... living standards should only be maintained to a lower level, for three main reasons:

They tend to be regarded as 'responsible' for their unemployed state

It would provide the essential motivation for continuing to look for a job

More help should be directed to low-paid workers

People's views on the treatment of the unemployed represent a compromise between their desire for humane treatment of the genuine individual and their instinct that the non-genuine should be discriminated against...

(Schlackman 1978, viii to ix)

In effect, the unemployed individual always seems to be somehow suspect: at best he is seen as probably in part to blame for his unemployment; and even if he is 'genuine' it is thought that he should be kept short, so that he keeps looking for work – otherwise there is the suspicion that he might just sit back and do nothing.

These issues are also touched on, but not fully reported, in a study of social trends, undertaken by S.S.R.C. Survey Unit in 1975 (*Social Trends*, 1976; see also Deacon, 1978). We know of other work which will reflect public opinion, but which is currently still in the field. We may have missed some articles, for instance under the aegis of 'social administration', whose titles did not alert us that they dealt with public opinion and the unemployed: and we have almost certainly missed, due to their ephemeral nature, answers to occasional questions about the unemployed in occasional public opinion surveys published by the media. The basic fact, however, is that we were able to locate only one empirical study of public opinion of the unemployed which explored that opinion in any detail – and that was a small study, not readily available.

The American literature is only a little richer. Even there, the few articles which we found were not explicitly and solely concerned with attitudes towards the unemployed, but rather with attitudes to the provision of 'welfare', and to the recipients of it; and this encompasses the needy of all kinds, even if the unemployed do form a large proportion of these. Typical of such studies and more 'psychological' than most are Ogren (1973), Williamson (1974), and perhaps especially Osgood (1977), who compares urban and rural attitudes, and provides a useful brief review of other related American research. This kind of work seems to have yielded two main findings. First, attitudes to people who are 'on welfare' depend on personal values and possibly on personality, but do not seem to be closely correlated with socio-economic status: the poor and near poor are as likely to be 'puritanical' about welfare as the well-to-do; the well-to-do are as likely to be 'liberal' as the poor. Secondly, and from a social psychological standpoint potentially more interesting, people who live in cities seem to be more sympathetic to the provision of welfare, and to the recipients of it, than people in the rural areas (Osgood, 1977). These findings may appear to contradict those of Kasl and his colleagues which we cited earlier (Kasl *et al.*, 1975; Gore, 1978). To recapitulate, Kasl's group found that it was the men made redundant in *rural* areas who received good social support, rather than those made redundant in the city. The contradiction between Kasl's and Osgood's results is however almost certainly a product of their very different methodologies: Osgood's derived from a re-analysis of answers to questions in opinion surveys, couched in terms of stereotypes such as 'most welfare recipients...'; Kasl's were based on the unemployed men themselves, men who would have been personally known in the community as sound people, as good workers. What we have, therefore, is that the anonymous stereotype is regarded with more sympathy in the anonymous city than in the country; in the country the 'type' is indeed looked down upon, but the more easily known and personally credible individual receives more practical support; by the same token, the local lay-abouts proper are, of course, also more visible, and it is they who come to represent the type.

In the end, however, there is very little research-based evidence on what *ordinary* people *actually* think and feel about the unemployed. To off-set this there is the consolation that 'public opinion' is, of course, only very tenuously connected with the opinion of individual members of the public: it is not some amalgam of the opinions of a numerical majority, but rather that of those sections of society which are most motivated and influential on the issue in question (see Blumer, 1962, for a classic discussion of this problem). 'Public opinion' in this sense, part technical and part popular, has three characteristics which are particularly important for our present analysis. First, it is rarely concerned with matters of fact, it is mostly concerned with programmes for action: whether or not Unidentified Flying Objects come from outer space would scarcely be considered a question of, or for, public opinion; but what to do about them if they do, would be. Secondly, from a different but closely related perspective, public opinion is rarely concerned with what *is*, it is mostly concerned with what *should* be: in effect, it is a response to perceived discrepancies between expectations (or aspirations) and reality (it is also for this reason that public opinion may sometimes become concerned with what is, because what is may be seen as what should be, and this may appear to be threatened by what might come to be). Thirdly, 'public opinion' has long been culturally endowed with a certain moral authority; and so demands for action can be justified in the name of 'public opinion', and actions attributable to it can be presented as legitimate.

The richest sources of evidence on public opinion of the unemployed are the ways in which the unemployed are treated in the media; the extent to which society makes provision for them through the offices of the state; and, within this, the manifold of conditions on which alone that provision can be obtained. The raw material potentially available from these sources is enormous: encompassing television, radio, and the press, and the regulations and publications of government, it constitutes a literature (not always exactly literate) of its own.

There is one exceptional overview and analysis of one very important facet of all this, namely of the 'Scrounging Controversy' of the 1970s, by Deacon (1978). This includes numerous quotations on the problems of scroungers and on the needs and methods to eliminate them, taken from the media, government sources, and politicians generally. Deacon also examines the roots of the controversy in the 1920s, both in that article and, in more detail, in an earlier brief monograph which covers the period 1920 to 1931 (Deacon, 1976). He ultimately attributes 'scrounger-phobia', as he calls it, to the general decline in living standards, which eroded differentials in after-tax income between the unemployed and those at work, especially the many relatively lower paid. Although he does not use the term, his implicit model is social comparison theory (Festinger, 1954; see also Patchen, 1961). One implication of this is that 'scrounger-phobia' can _not_ be simply attributed to the media and to politicians. Referring to the results of the 1975 S.S.R.C. Survey, he reports that

'make people work' and 'stop social security abuses' was accorded a higher priority than crime, strikes, taxation, immigration, or world peace – even though the national newspapers were carrying few stories of abuse at the time of the survey. (Deacon, 1978, p. 127)

According to Deacon, concern with abuse came in third place as 'the ONE thing you would most like to change to improve the Quality Of Life in Britain today' (Deacon refers to personal communication on this issue; we have not seen the actual figures ourselves). One response to this was more checks to see if the claimant was perhaps working on the side, or, if not, if he was genuinely looking for work,

We need the element of surprise, the spot check, the unexpected interview, the off-beat home visit. (quoted Deacon, 1978, p. 134)

It was 1976; it was a Labour government; the speaker was Stan Orme, somewhat on the left of that party.

Deacon's account of the scrounging controversy, his examination of its history, the sources which he quotes and to which he points, are all most valuable. In the final analysis, however, his perspective is from the standpoint of social administration: he is not a psychologist; he is not concerned with psychological problems; he does not ask psychological questions. Yet there are clearly very important psychological, and particularly social psychological, questions to be asked. Going back to the 1920s, Deacon himself remarks,

> some three-million claimants were refused benefit on the grounds that they were not genuinely seeking work, although at no time in these years did anyone seriously suggest that the work which they were supposed to be seeking actually existed.                                          (Deacon, 1978, p. 125)

Though the 1970s and the 1980s have not seen this extent of refusal of benefit, the underlying pattern is unchanged: well before actual refusal, the justification for *low* levels of benefit is to provide the incentive to look for work, even though it is perfectly well understood that for the majority of unemployed the work is not there to be found. There is a simple, but important, psychological question here: *why*? In almost any other imaginable situation, persistent pursuit of the unlikely, the *demonstrably* unlikely, would be discouraged, even laughed at, however sympathetically: it would scarcely ever continue to be encouraged, let alone insisted upon. It would, after all, be 'unrealistic'. It would be like persisting with a wage claim when there plainly is no money to meet it: bans on over-time, going-slow, strikes, would be seen as irrational, certainly by objective observers. And in practice they would be self-defeating. Yet much like this happens in relation to an individual who is unemployed. There is the insistence that he continues to look for work, though it is known that there is almost none to be had: stringent use of regulations to put pressure on him has much in common with 'working-to-rule': ultimately, just as the worker can withhold his labour, so the state can in effect go 'on strike' by withholding benefits. In the end here, too, the process is often self-defeating: for pressure to find work, followed by repeated rejection, and subsistence levels of living, so undermine the mental and physical condition of the individual that employers are reluctant to entrust him with a job, even when they have one.

There are no doubt other comparisons to be made. The central fact is that by any normal criteria of what is reasonable and realistic – by the same criteria which, for example, animate public opinion in relation to wage claims and strikes – public opinion, and the behaviour of the state towards the unemployed which it underwrites, are quite manifestly unrealistic. We have deliberately used the term 'state', because party of government may make a difference in points of detail, but the basic approach has long been above party politics. Nor can it be said that the state is in this respect out of touch with the people. There is this to add to the Schlackman study and the S.S.R.C. Survey,

In November 1976 Jon Akass wrote an article in *The Sun*, asking for 'real evidence' of abuse. The letters *poured* in
> 'There are an astonishing number of people prepared to denounce their friends and inlaws as scroungers, which seems to show that slander – like murder – is mostly a family crime.' (quoted Deacon, 1978, p. 131)

One ostensible psychological explanation for this unrealistic approach might be that our economy and society are in a period of transition: our approach is unrealistic because we are confronted with a quite new situation. We are not: that explanation, therefore, will not do. Deacon's comments on the 1920s, for instance, can be found in almost so many words more than a hundred years earlier, in a report of a Parliamentary Committee on the Poor Laws of 1817. First there is the evidence of Castlereagh

for if no means could be found 'of inspiring the population with the wish to live rather on their own labour than what they could draw from the property and labour of others', he firmly believed that the English people would not in future ages be what they had been in the past. (Nicholls, 1854/1966, vol. II, p. 168)

The Committee itself, however, reported on

the impossibility of always providing employment for all who may be in want of it . . . 'to hold out to the labouring classes that all who require it shall be provided with work at adequate wages is therefore to lead them to false views of their position' . . . (Nicholls, 1854/1966, vol. II, p. 174)

Essentially the same pattern has recurred and been recognised for centuries for example in relation to enclosures (e.g. Eden, 1795). If it takes that long for a society to come to terms with change, that itself requires psychological explanation (for a fuller discussion see Kelvin, 1984).

The truth is, of course, much more complicated, and we can only begin to explore it. First, most readers will have been edgy for several pages by the apparent one-sidedness of our account. They will know from their own experience that there is not only scrounger-hounding but also widespread sympathy for the unemployed, and often anger on their behalf and at the ways in which they are treated. Our apparent one-sidedness so far stems from a bias in the literature. The *literature* has been motivated by concern for the unemployed, and its attention has therefore inevitably concentrated on the mean and demeaning aspects of the treatment of the unemployed: that holds not only for the major contributions of Deacon (1976; 1978), but also for the host of smaller ones of a more generalist kind (e.g. Emmett, 1977; Field, 1977a; Golding and Middleton, 1978; Field,

1974; Douglas, 1980; Atkinson and Trinder, 1981). We do not know of any study which has collated, analysed and commented on manifestations of support for the unemployed: on the editorials and articles critical of government policy (Labour as well as Conservative); or the attempts to shame the lay scrounger-hounders as Jon Akass clearly intended; or the many documentary programmes and television plays which have explored the plight of being unemployed; or the radio stations which run services to find work. As a species we thrive on negative feed-back: but the positive side, the concern, is just as much a feature of society's reaction to the unemployed, and as much part of their environment, as is scrounger-hunting.

The social psychological problem is to try to account for this ambivalence of society, of public opinion. To talk of 'public opinion' as 'ambivalent' is not to reify it or, more strictly, to personify it. It is not that public opinion is 'divided', so that one section is all scrounger-hounding, the other all sympathy. There are no doubt extremists of this kind on this issue, as on every other. Such evidence as there is, however, reflects a largely unresolved confusion of *both* themes. The confusion can be seen in the Schlackman study, even though its overall pattern tilts towards scrounger-hounding. The mix is manifest in the behaviour of the media and the speeches of politicians, which alternate in their indignation of scroungers and at the problems of the unemployed. It is not an adequate answer to say that 'of course' everyone has sympathy for the unemployed, and that it is only the few scroungers who spoil everything and have to be rooted out. This might seem plausible in theory: in practice it has led to attitudes and behaviour which in any other context would be regarded as unrealistic; and so preoccupation with the scrounging few has distorted the system of providing for the great majority for whom there is a genuine sympathy. Where a pattern of responding is so excessive in relation to its cause, and so unrealistic in its nature, there are psychological questions to be asked.

There is a third theme, the theme of the Protestant Work Ethic. This is a curious and, from a social psychological standpoint, a very important phenomenon. It is not public opinion in the same sense as, say, public opinion that scroungers must be punished, or that unemployment is a great waste of human potential. The Protestant Work Ethic, or rather the *concept* of this Ethic, refers to beliefs and values at a higher level of abstraction or generality, which, as it were, inform particular opinions – on, for example, scrounging. The first curious feature of this is that initially, the concept of the Protestant Ethic was, of course, a highly academic notion, put forward by Weber 1904–5, and 'for all its fame the *Protestant Ethic* is a fragment ... much shorter and less detailed than Weber's other studies of "religions"' (Giddens, 1976, p. 5). Weber himself was quite tentative, and the validity of the concept was questioned from the very beginning. Nevertheless, throughout the twentieth century, and especially in recent years, the Protestant Ethic, or its secular heir, the Work Ethic, has been repeatedly invoked to 'explain' attitudes to work, to unemployment, to the unemployed.

there is no doubt in the relationship between Protestantism and the importance attributed to work. The Protestant Ethic lives on in secularised form, insofar as the prevalent cultural norms attribute status and dignity to the worker, who is seen as a fully fledged and contributing member of society, and denies the same things to the non-worker.                    (Hayes and Nutman, 1981, p. 4)

The 'cultural norm' of a Protestant Work Ethic has been widely assumed, and treated as self-evident. Now and again one can find a study which questions, not so much whether the Ethic exists, but at least in what form it does so, and then actually investigates this empirically (Goldstein and Eichorn, 1961). In other writing the Ethic is taken for granted: at best some 'measure' of it is occasionally used as the independent variable in the study of, say, attitudes to work; more usually it is simply introduced as a vague explanatory concept (e.g. Blood, 1969; Mirels and Garrett, 1971; Stone, 1975; Greenberg, 1978; Albee, 1977; Anthony, 1977: see also Furnham, 1982). To these more-or-less scholarly uses of the Protestant Ethic have to be added its use as little more than an incantation by the media, trade unionists, industrialists, journalists, politicians, and all and sundry once they have heard of it: we are conditioned by it; we must return to its traditional values, or free ourselves from this out-dated heritage – and so on:

The Work Ethic is so deeply ingrained in British and other industrialised societies that work has acquired a value in itself, even though it is widely regarded as unpleasant.                    (Jenkins and Sherman, 1979, p. 2)

It may well be that in the next 10, 15, or 20 years we will have a new philosophy towards unemployment. We may have to move away from the Protestant Work Ethic.          (James Prior, M.P., quoted in *The Guardian*, 22 March 1979)

In effect, the Protestant Work Ethic is no longer just an idea discussed by academics, it has become part of public opinion. It has become so mainly because those who write and talk about 'public opinion' regularly explain that opinion in terms of the Work Ethic; and in doing so they have disseminated the *concept* of this Ethic. Repeated recourse to the Protestant Work Ethic as an 'explanation' has thus made it into a self-fulfilling prophesy; it has become a generally accepted way of looking at the unemployed and their problems – and one which, as we shall see, the unemployed have widely come to accept in evaluating themselves.

The reader will be aware that we have grave reservations. When one explores the evidence, it becomes very doubtful indeed whether there is a cultural norm of a Work Ethic, Protestant or otherwise. It is even more doubtful if there ever was such a norm. Yet it is precisely its *assumed* deep roots in history ('culture') which are perceived as the source of its continuing power. In fact, the Protestant Work Ethic is a classic example of a *myth*: it is not a wholly false account of the past, but a highly selective and distorted one, whose function is not to describe and explain the past itself, but to inspire the present (Kelvin, 1984). From the standpoint of a given individual it matters very little whether his behaviour is shaped by myth or by what is indeed a long-standing cultural norm. It does matter at a social psychological level of explanation. It is one thing to explain something as the *product* of a myth, it is quite another to take the myth itself as the explanation. If one explains behaviour by something recognised as a myth, this does not prevent the search for alternative, valid explanations; on the contrary it is likely to encourage it. If however one accepts the myth as the truth, one is unlikely to look further; one's explanations will therefore be at best inadequate and probably misleading. Since the Protestant Work Ethic has been so constantly invoked as an explanation at the psychological level of analysis, its status as fact or myth is of fundamental importance.

In terms of its psychological characteristics, the concept of an 'ethic' refers to a system of values which the members of a group, sect, or society have internalised, so that actions based upon it may be regarded as acts of choice. In other words, acts based on an ethic are acts which the individual wants to do in their own right, and not because they are forced upon him by an external circumstance. Bearing in mind, then, that the great bulk of our society is supposed to have been permeated by a Work Ethic for generations, the essential facts seem to be these. The sixteenth and especially the seventeenth centuries saw the economic rise of a *section* of the middle class which was genuinely inspired by a sense of the religious significance of work, and of frugality in their personal lives – what Weber called 'asceticism': and so the profits from work were not to be used to indulge in luxuries, or to retire from work, but to create more work, and thereby more opportunities for serving God. On that basis alone, anyone who believes that ours is, or ever predominantly was, a society rooted in the Protestant Work Ethic has failed to understand its most essential teaching: for the one thing which the Protestant Work Ethic would *not* have tolerated is that productivity should increase the profits, wages, and luxuries of some, at the cost of unemployment for others. However, these values and sentiments were never more than those of a minority, and of middle-class rather than working- or upper-class origin. The notion that the generality of English workers were imbued with this Ethic just does not survive examination. For at least the last five hundred years, there is steady and consistent evidence of late coming to work, long breaks at work, early leaving of work, downing of tools at the first opportunity, and the like distain for work (Kelvin, 1984). To take one example: in the 1860s, at the height of that reputedly so marvellously industrious Victorian England, and at its very centre, Birmingham:

An enormous amount of time is lost, not only by want of punctuality in coming to work in the morning and the beginning again after meals, but still more by the general observation of 'St Monday' . . . One employer has on Monday only 40 or 50 out of 300 or 400.

(Parliamentary Papers, 1884; cited Royston Pyke, 1967, p. 88)

The fifteenth-century version (1495) reads:

Divers artificers and labourers waste much part of the day in the late coming to work, early departing there from, long sitting at their breakfast, at their dinner and . . . long sleeping afternoon. (cited Coleman, 1966, p. 303)

And these were not factory workers alienated by the division of labour, but that elite of mediaeval craftsmen, the masons, working on Canterbury Cathedral.

Furthermore, the English worker was typically not a church- or chapel-goer in what in any case had long not been the church- and chapel-going society of another popular myth. From at least the eighteenth century, the growth of the towns, and therefore the reduced surveillance of and social pressures on the individual, led to a fall in religious attendance which greatly worried non-conformists, as well as the established church. It was not a problem simply solved by the building of more churches. In the historically unique census of attendance of 1851, which covered *all* denominations, 'in a score of the largest towns in England fewer than one person in ten . . . attended *any* place of worship on Census Sunday' (Inglis, 1964, p. 2), and the most industrial areas were the least religious (Hobsbawm, 1968). In the 1880s, Mears found that, for example, of 2,290 people living in Bow Common, only 135 ever attended any place of worship, and of those 47 were children – and so on (Keating, 1976). A good case has in fact been made that in becoming a church- or chapel-goer, the artisan or labourer 'hardly seemed any longer a member of the working class' (Chadwick, 1975, p. 102). The idea that any substantial body of the working class has at any time worked with a sense of religious calling is arrant nonsense: the vast majority have always done so simply to make their living. So much also for religion as the opium of the people. As for the 'masters', the predominant ideal amongst these was not that of the Protestant Work Ethic, but of the 'gentleman': the gentleman who perhaps tended his estates, who would be expected to cultivate worthwhile pursuits, but who would not, ideally, have to work at all; and if he should need to earn his living, it would be in one of the learned professions – the law or the church, and possibly medicine (but perhaps not surgery, which was rather dirty, and so was left to barbers). With the coming of manufacturing industry, the entrepreneur typically sought to become landed: and although he could never quite become a 'gentleman' himself, he would seek to establish his son as such and marry his daughter to one (Jones, 1967). For the fact is that, in England, to stay in trade, however successfully, is to remain forever at the side-door of society.

When one looks at the situation from the very historical perspective which ostensibly gave rise to it, explanations in terms of the Protestant Ethic emerge as little more than an invention of twentieth-century social science, with unwarranted pretensions to an ancient lineage. The 'ethic' which has truly been predominant and pervasive is not a work ethic but, for want of a better term, a *wealth ethic*. Wealth is (quite correctly) perceived as the basis of economic independence: *that* is the key issue, and has been so for centuries. The 'ethic' is to make or to have sufficient wealth not to have to depend on others; work is only one means to that end, and certainly not the one universally most esteemed: not in any class. Provided that one has money enough to be independent, there is no great moral obligation to work, certainly not in the sense of gainful, productive employment. Literary evidence, say Jane Austen, suggests that one might be expected to develop such talents as one may have, and to contribute socially in a variety of voluntary ways; and in families which are old as well as wealthy, there is often a long tradition of public service. All this, however, stems far more from a classical education than from Christian teaching: its roots are the Athens of Plato and Aristotle, rather than the prescriptions of seventeenth-century Puritanism. The rest, even if they *also* gain numerous other satisfactions from work, work for the money, and the things which money enables them to have and to do. Within *this* ethic, the problem of the unemployed is not that they are 'idle', but that they are poor. The difference matters, especially from a psychological standpoint, and the myth of the Protestant Work Ethic has obscured it. In the final analysis, explanations in terms of an ethic rest on the distinction between the 'good' and the 'bad': explanations based on poverty rest on the distinctions between the 'haves' and the 'have-nots'. The 'bad' we are entitled to disapprove of, ostracise, punish; the 'have-nots' we know from our most basic ethic we ought to help. We have a psychologically vested interest in explanations in terms of the Protestant Work Ethic. Given our picture of ourselves as fundamentally moral, it is much more congenial to us to attribute our attitudes to the unemployed as 'conditioned' by an ethic, than as motivated by meanness. The inescapable fact, however, is that the have-nots are dependent for their material survival on contributions from others either in the form of private charity or of provision from the public purse: and resentment at having to feed, clothe, and shelter the bodies of the unemployed poor has long aroused far more public passion than has concern for the salvation of souls of the leisured rich.

The underlying pattern of public opinion and attitudes towards the unemployed goes back to the Ordinance of Labourers of 1349, in the reign of Edward III. This is not the place, and we do not have the expertise, to trace in detail all that has happened since: *that* is amply documented and explored in the large literature on Poor Law. Certain very basic aspects of that history are, however, directly relevant to our concerns – in the same sense as the concept of the Protestant Work Ethic would have been, if it had been valid. It is this Ordinance which distinguishes between 'sturdy beggars', who were fit for work and, in effect, the 'deserving poor', that is the sick, those too old or too young, or otherwise too infirm to work: and it forbade, on penalty of imprisonment, the giving of arms to 'sturdy beggars . . . so that they may be compelled to labour for the necessities of life' (the words of the Ordinance, Bland *et al.*, 1914, p. 166). Ever since then, thought and action concerning the unemployed has fundamentally been shaped by these concepts of 'sturdy beggar' and 'deserving poor'. This has had two main consequences. First, since only the inadequate were deserving, to be genuinely 'deserving' implied some inadequacy, whether of body or mind, or both. Secondly, in order to ensure that sturdy beggars be truly and effectively discouraged, the conditions for obtaining poor relief were made deeply unpleasant, even for the deserving. The Elizabethan Poor Laws were a partial exception to this in that they were interventionist, and required parishes to act positively by providing work (the Younger Pitt, the 'father' of modern Toryism, but clearly something of a 'wet', also had an interventionist scheme, but had to withdraw it in face of opposition). Intervention is costly: the dominant policy, therefore, was to demean and shame the poor. The age of Newton and of Locke, for example, produced this 1697 Act of William III

that the money raised only for the relief of such as are as well impotent and poor, may not be misapplied and consumed by the idle, sturdy and disorderly beggars . . . every such person upon relief . . . and the wife and children of any such person . . . shall upon the shoulder of the right sleeve of the uppermost garment . . . in an open and visible manner, wear such a badge or mark . . . a large RP, together with the first letter of the parish . . . cut in blue or red cloth.

(8 and 9. Wm. 3.30. 1697 [*sic*]: cited Eden, 1797, appendix cixxvi)

A century later:

Badging the poor is supposed to have been of service in reducing the rates.

(Eden, 1796, p. 145)

as was the prospect of the workhouse:

The parish generally insists on the poor going into the workhouse; by which expenditure is much reduced: not because the poor are maintained at a cheaper rate in the house than they could be in their own homes, but because apprehension of being obliged to intermix with the various description of indigent people usually found in a large Poor-house, deters many from making applications for relief . . . It seems to bear hard upon the modest poor, who are the most deserving of national charity.                                                    (Eden, 1797, p. 228)

The workhouse-as-deterrent finally became an instrument of national policy with the Poor Law of 1834, which stipulated that conditions there should be 'less eligible' than those which would be available from the meanest wage. The policy was unworkable in the context of nineteenth-century manufacturing industry, and its harshness became increasingly offensive to public opinion: and late in that century, and early in the twentieth, unemployment came to be recognised as a special problem, which could not be tackled simply within Poor Law, but required measures in its own right (Beveridge, 1909/31). This brings us to the complexities of the present. Material provision for the unemployed – as for all who would once have been called 'The Poor' – is now incomparably better than 50, let alone 150, years ago. Similarly, public degradation and shaming of the poor as an explicit instrument of public policy is clearly something of the past. These changes themselves reflect the much greater sympathy of public opinion in relation to people in need. (From the standpoint of the unemployed, the vast number of regulations, and the manner in which they are applied, may seem degrading, and may be so subjectively: but it is important not to mistake the pettiness of a self-regarding bureaucracy, and of *some* of its officials, as basic public policy.) In relation to the unemployed in particular, however, the situation remains fundamentally problematic, the problem being the traditional problem of the 'sturdy beggar'.

Some distinction between 'sturdy beggars' and the 'deserving poor', that is between 'scroungers' and 'genuine cases', is both necessary (at least psychologically) and wholly justified: and genuine claimants are often very anxious that it should be made, in order to maintain the integrity of their own standing (which is also not to be ignored psychologically). The critical factor is the *criterion* which defines 'deserving' or 'genuine'. This is where matters have gone awry; and to understand what has happened it is essential to go back to the Ordinance of Labourers with which it all began.

One of the most significant features of the Ordinance was that it proscribed the *giving* of alms: until then one of the most basic cultural norms enjoined on mediaeval man was the dispensing of charity to the poor, all conditions of poor. Mediaeval man was probably no better than we are, but the teaching of the church on charity was unequivocal, and the blessing of the church was deemed important. The Ordinance, which ran so utterly counter to this (hence, presumably the threat to *punish* the giving of alms) was a response to a deep crisis: the devastation of the Black Death of 1347/8. The Ordinance opens:

Because a great part of the people, and especially of workmen and servants has now died in this plague . . .                                   (Bland *et al.*, 1914, p. 164)

Plague had reduced the available work-force by between one-third to one-half. Anyone who could work was desperately needed: not to work could only be countenanced on the ground that the individual was not fit. The fundamental criterion was simply physical and mental fitness for work. This criterion was perfectly rational and defensible in the conditions in which it evolved, when there was a grave *shortage of labour*, when there was plenty of work, and the need for every available hand: it is *not* appropriate for conditions in which there is a very serious *shortage of work*, so that even those fit and eager to do it cannot find it. Yet that is what has happened: in essence we are handling a problem of the late twentieth century with conceptual tools fashioned in the fourteenth, and for purposes opposite to our own. This has had a very important effect on the way in which the unemployed individual is seen, and sees himself. If the condition is one of plenty of work in relation to available labour, an individual's unemployment can only be explained by something about his *person*: he (or she) is physically or mentally too unfit to cope with work, or too idle (being rich would not, on its own, be regarded as sufficient). If, on the other hand, the condition is one of shortage of work in relation to labour, the individual may also and indeed more probably would be unemployed because of the general *economic* situation: at the very least, under the circumstances there are three possible explanations for an individual's unemployment, not just two.

Our present condition is manifestly and admittedly of the second kind, and most unemployment is recognised to be due to situational factors. However, when we talk of the 'unemployed' as people, rather than of 'unemployment' as an economic phenomenon, our *language* is still predominantly derived from the Ordinance of Labourers, and its distinctions in terms of personal qualities. In particular 'desert' or 'genuineness' implies some form of inadequacy. The poor or unemployed used to receive 'relief', or 'assistance', or 'National Assistance', supplemented by 'allowances'. Currently they receive 'benefit', in this context meaning 'pecuniary assistance' (*Shorter Oxford English Dictionary*), or 'allowance' (*Concise Oxford English Dictionary*): 'allowance' is itself used in two senses, as in 'limited supply', and as in 'mitigating circumstances' (*Concise Oxford English Dictionary*). The whole set of connotations is that of providing a limited amount of help for those who cannot quite cope by themselves – and, by implication, anyone who could help himself has no right to 'relief', 'assistance', 'allowances', 'benefit', or whatever else the label for provision from the public purse. From one objective standpoint all this is quite correct and justified: either the individual cannot cope, and thus deserves support; or else he can, and has no grounds to look for free gifts from his fellows. Within this, however, it is still necessary to ask *why* the individual cannot cope, and here, the heritage of the Ordinance of Labourers, and its exclusive concern with personal qualities, obscures the role of situational factors – the individual was *made* unable to cope, because his job came to an end, and he continues to be unable to cope, because he cannot find another. Though it is obviously no more than an *ad hominem* argument, we ask the reader to consider the implications of talking, not in terms of unemployment 'assistance' or 'benefit', but of unemployment *'compensation'*: 'compensation' clearly implies that the onus is on others, or on the situation, not on the unemployed individual. This is not a new idea: John Stuart Mill pleaded that

there cannot be a more legitimate object of the legislator's care than the interests of those who are thus sacrificed to the gains of their fellow citizens and posterity.
(quoted Beveridge, 1909/31, pp. 12–13, source not given)

Or, in an equally succinct modern version

It is only fair that the rest of the community should pay and pay generously, to maintain those who have to carry the burden of this transition directly.
(Enoch Powell, on the unemployed, quoted *The Times*, 6 September 1980)

There is evidence of movement in that direction. A relatively new term in the language of unemployment is 'redundancy', and redundancy is indeed often linked with 'compensation'. Even here, however, the tug of the personal becomes ultimately irresistible: though it is the economic or technological situation which caused the redundancy, it is the individual who carries the label 'redundant' – implying someone who is no longer useful and, to that extent, inadequate.

Perhaps the one term to date which is predominantly situational is 'jobless', which is at once more precisely descriptive than 'unemployed' or 'out of work', and in which the suffix '-less' at least suggests that the situation described is not quite normal. This is a very recent term: it is not included in the 1976 edition of the *Concise Oxford English Dictionary*;

among the main Oxford series its first appearance seems to be in the Oxford paper-back dictionary of 1979; that is only a rough guide, of course, but it is an indication.

The fundamental problem concerning public opinion about the unemployed is to understand its ambiguity and ambivalence. Singly the most prevalent explanation, or hypothesis, has been based on the Protestant Work Ethic – that is, on the assumption that this Ethic is indeed very potent, but no longer appropriate to the technological economies of our age. We hope we have shown that the Protestant Work Ethic is very largely a myth: that for the vast majority of people work is, and always has been, a matter of labouring 'for the necessities or life'. Work may be a *norm*, but it is not an *ethic*: it is 'expected' on the good statistical ground of its very high incidence, not on the basis of its moral significance. Moral significance does not attach to work as such, but to 'not living off others'; the only exception being weakness of body or mind so that one cannot work because of one's inadequacy. That, we have argued, has its roots in the fourteenth-century dichotomy of the concepts of 'sturdy beggar' and 'the deserving poor'. There are therefore at least two possible explanations for the ambivalence of public opinion on the unemployed: in terms of an outdated ethic and in terms of an outdated language. These are not incompatible alternatives: on the contrary, the Protestant Work Ethic could be seen as underwriting the concepts of the language of unemployment, and the language as ossifying the concepts of the Ethic. There is some substance in this, but the language of unemployment almost certainly accounts for rather more of the phenomena than the Ethic, both historically and psychologically. Public opinion is a product of communication, with language as its most important medium. The language of unemployment defines the issues which are available for public discussion, through the terms in which that discussion is conducted. Furthermore, as we showed earlier, unemployment and the unemployed constitute the kind of complex and therefore ambiguous problem on which the individual generally feels in need of the opinion of others to clarify his own. 'Public opinion', as he perceives it, thus very largely defines the issues for the individual, even if he himself does not wholly share that opinion. The language of unemployment is not the dominant cause of the social psychological problems of unemployment; but its inadequacy, due to its out-datedness, may be a major check on solving them.

# 7   'Others'

There remain two questions which at first seem rather different but in practice are closely connected: 'how does his unemployment affect the way in which the unemployed individual sees other people?', and 'how does it affect the way in which he perceives himself to be seen *by* others?'. The two questions are closely related because the way in which an individual regards others is inevitably much affected by how, as he sees it, *they* regard him. There is nothing unique here in the situation of the unemployed: it happens whenever an individual, for whatever reason, becomes conscious of his own status, and believes that that status is relevant to others – or that it would be or should be relevant to them, if they were aware of it. The connection is, however, especially close for the unemployed. Unemployment creates numerous ambiguities and uncertainties. The typical response to uncertainty and ambiguity is to make the individual more than usually aware of himself and his position; and as a result it also makes him take much more notice than usually of any cues which others may provide, and which may clarify his situation. We have discussed all this at length already. The fact is that unemployment produces precisely the kind of psychological conditions in which the individual is likely to be particularly sensitive to how he believes he is regarded by others; and the way in which he perceives himself to be seen by others will tend to be particularly important for how he in turn sees them. This state of heightened self-awareness may not last indefinitely, but it clearly lasts long enough not to be fully outgrown within the span of any accounts of the unemployed (for example, Bakke, 1933; Marsden and Duff, 1975; and Swinburn, 1981).

The unemployed do, of course, also have a relatively more objective view of others, as it were in their own right: indeed it is only inasmuch as the unemployed can see others as such that they can use them as a standard against which they compare their own lot. At this point we have to differentiate within that so far vague and amorphous body of 'others'. One group amongst these, the unemployed individual's fellow unemployed, constitute a special class of problems which we shall set aside until towards the end. The remaining 'others' – by implication either employed or at least not to be counted among 'the unemployed' – can be divided into three main categories. First there are, for want of a better term, 'people at large': these are the generality of people whom one passes in the street, whom one may overhear talking in a shop; in effect all the people whom one does not actually know but who, as an aggregated abstract, are the 'they' of 'they say', 'they think', 'they treat you . . .'; they are the 'generalised other' postulated in symbolic interactionism. The second category consists of others with whom one has some form of personal relationship – one's family, friends, acquaintances. This leaves as a third group those others with whom one has a purely functional relationship, especially the staffs of Benefit Offices and other agencies, employers, and 'contacts' who are not friends or family.

There is no solid evidence on any of this, not in the sense of evidence derived from research which was explicitly designed to explore the unemployed individual's perceptions of others, and his beliefs concerning their perception of him. (The nearest to a systematic study of this kind is perhaps Komarovsky's analysis of authority relationships within unemployed families: Komarovsky, 1940). There is, however, a considerable amount of incidental evidence, both direct and indirect, in the autobiographical accounts and case studies of the unemployed, such as Beales and Lambert (1934), Gould and Kenyon (1972), Bakke (1933), Zawadski and Lazarsfeld (1935), Marsden and Duff (1975), Briar (1977), Hill (1978), and in passing references in many other places (e.g. Cohen, 1972; Campling, 1978; Fagin, 1980). At this level the list of possible references to the odd telling remark or anecdote is almost endless: it is rather more useful to consider the main themes.

As far as 'they' are concerned, in their own right, there are two main themes. First, 'they' just don't know how lucky they are: they have somewhere to go each day, something to do; they have some sort of recognised place in society and self-respect; they have money, and can do things. Secondly, and closely related to the first, 'they' don't understand: they don't understand what it is like *not* to have anything to do, *not* to have money, *not* to have a place in society; they don't know what it is like to feel that one has let down one's family, what it is like to be repeatedly rejected by employers, to be mucked about and have one's personal life scrutinised by officials no better than oneself.

The unemployed individual's picture of others as 'lucky' is scarcely surprising. It is no answer to this that sometimes he could find a job if he were prepared to change his trade or to work for relatively lowly wages. At the very least that itself makes those who do not have to face this dilemma luckier than himself: and in many instances, where the poverty trap operates, to take a job at wages less than benefits would involve sacrifices for his family; so he quite genuinely sometimes swallows his pride and takes benefits (Schlackman Research Organisation Ltd, 1978). There are good objective grounds on which most of the unemployed might well envy the 'luck' of those with jobs.

There is also an important subjective reason, implicit in the notion of 'luck' as such. Being lucky has nothing to do with being better; on the contrary, it denies the relevance of abilities or qualities. In seeing others as 'lucky', the unemployed individual not only compares his fortune with theirs, but also implies that the differences between him and them are largely outside the control of *either*. The essence of this was embodied in the fictional Yosser Hughes, the unemployed, deeply disturbed, central character of a B.B.C. television play of 1982: on seeing others at work he would repeatedly say 'I can do that; give us a job' (Bleasdale, 1982). From the standpoint of the unemployed, but for the luck of the devil, or the grace of God, those with and those without jobs are largely interchangeable. A lucky man is by no means necessarily a better man. The distinction is very important to the self-concept of the unemployed. To see the world in terms of external locus of control is not a manifestation of a basic personality trait, nor is it necessarily even the result of actual experience: the unemployed have a very understandable vested interest in taking this stance, in order to preserve their self-respect (Rotter, 1966; Lefcourt, 1976). Conversely, others have a vested interest in the hypothesis of the *Just World* (Lerner, 1976), whereby the victim, however innocent in fact, is still felt to be at least partly to blame for his fate; and, as we noted earlier, 'others' do drift quite quickly into feeling that somehow the unemployed individual is at least partly to blame for his unemployment – even when they know perfectly well, rationally, that it is first and foremost a product of macro-economic factors.

The other main theme of the unemployed individual's perception of others is that others simply 'don't understand' what it is like to be unemployed: that one does not want to be unemployed, that one would like to have work – and so on. This is, of course, where the perception of others merges inextricably with how they are believed to perceive oneself. To say 'they do not understand' is fundamentally to say 'they do not see me as I really am' which in fact reduces to 'how I see myself'. We shall return to this issue later in connection with the unemployed individual's sense of stigma. The most relevant psychological phenomenon in the present context is the implications of these apparently casual comments. Inasmuch as the unemployed individual sees others as *lucky*, in the sense of having been favoured by chance or fate, to that extent he lessens any implicit personal or moral distance between himself and those at work. Inasmuch as he perceives others as *not understanding*, he asserts a distance at a conceptual, cognitive level, which he then attributes to them, to their indifference, their insensitivity, their prejudice, or to some other failure of comprehension on *their* part.

Much of this perception of 'others' in general is inevitably also true of the unemployed individual's perception of his family and friends. What happens in the family is, as we have seen, almost wholly a function of the quality of family life before unemployment; where people loved and liked each other, unemployment, if anything, brings them closer; where they were falling apart, hostility increases, disintegration comes more swiftly, and probably more nastily. There are hints, for instance in Marsden and Duff (1975), of perhaps greater sensitivity to the wider family, for instance to in-laws: comments from in-laws which might have been ignored in 'normal' circumstances are resented, and it may well be of course that in-laws feel more free to show hostility to an unemployed individual which they had inhibited as long as he had a job. There is also the evidence (from Komarovsky, 1940, for example) that unemployed fathers and husbands feel that they have lost status with their wives and children: and there is evidence that unemployed husbands sometimes feel threatened if their wives have jobs when they have not (e.g. Marsden and Duff, 1975; Sinfield, 1981). One speculative conclusion, which may be worth considering, is that the unemployed individual resorts to more *stereotyped* expectations and criteria than he would use when he is in work. So in-laws come to be seen as more 'in-lawish'; children are expected to show more 'respect'; the domestic and dependent role of wives become even more salient. As we said, this is speculative, and much would no doubt depend on the degree to which relationships were already somewhat stereotypical prior to an individual's unemployment. Even quite generally, however, it would not be surprising if the unemployed individual saw his relations in more stereotypical forms than previously – at least for a time. The ambiguities and uncertainties of being unemployed create a need in the individual to reorientate and redefine himself. In the absence of work-related aspects of self-definition, some of the most important alternative sources of definition are probably in terms of conventional role relationships within the family, that is, in terms of stereotypes of roles and role partners – along the line of 'I'm still your father.'

The nature and quality of family relationships is so varied that any generalisations concerning the effects of unemployment upon them must be treated with great caution. As regards the unemployed individual's perception of his family and his beliefs about their perception of him only two generalisations are plausible, and even those two only tentatively. One is that unemployment will simply enhance however he saw his family and believed himself to be seen by them beforehand. The other is that it may enhance his tendency to see his family in terms of stereotypes. This last could then become the source of considerable tensions: it may raise far higher expectations of 'ideal' types of father, mother, husband, wife, and son and daughter, than would be entertained normally – and this just at a time when those ideals may be particularly difficult to even approximate.

The nature and quality of friendships is equally diverse, and here, too, generalisations must therefore be treated with much care. We shall leave for the moment the new friendships which the unemployed individual makes with other unemployed. Our immediate concern is with his perception of friends who go back to before his unemployment. Unemployment seems to sensitise the unemployed individual to the whole problem of *loyalty*, in a way in which he would probably have little occasion to be sensitised in normal circumstances. That is perhaps the one distinctive and fairly general effect of unemployment on friendship, though even this is not unique to unemployment: it arises in any major change of status, for instance on being widowed (Parkes, 1972). As the unemployed themselves see it, some friends stay friends, other friendships fade or come to an end altogether (Bakke, 1933; Komarovsky, 1940; Gould and Kenyon, 1972; Marsden and Duff, 1975; Briar, 1977). When one reads the comments of unemployed people on their friends, one gets the impression that the tone is set by the friends who have dropped away: their fickleness deeply hurts and angers the unemployed and makes the contrast of the steadfastness of remaining friends all the greater. The quality of loyalty – normally largely ignored because normally seldom required – thus becomes a very important dimension of friendship for the unemployed.

There are suggestions here and there that the unemployed see *some* of their former friends, but perhaps more so former acquaintances, as degrading them; and there is also evidence sometimes of a sense of being exploited. Experiences of degradation and of exploitation seem to occur mainly among unskilled or semi-skilled manual workers. For example, one of Marsden and Duff's unemployed men, and his wife, tell of a working men's club, which certainly allowed the unemployed to come in, but kept them apart on 'skid row', where they were occasionally treated to a glass of beer, and some stale, left-over pies (Marsden and Duff, 1975, p. 159). It may have been much better than that, and the intention of the working men may have been genuinely generous. In the present context, however, we are simply concerned with how the unemployed see such others – friends, acquaintances, fellow club-members: that often they seem to see themselves treated as hangers-on, as poor relations, as dependant.

Evidence of exploitation spans nearly fifty years, from Bakke (1933) to Marsden and Duff (1975) and the Schlackman Research Organisation Ltd (1978). It arises from a mixture of placation and bribery by the unemployed in search of work. Finding work is very often a matter of having contacts; the contacts are very often in the pub, where, at the very least, they are receptive to the offer of a drink; and by no means infrequently, there is perhaps money to be passed to the contact, to the ganger, or foreman, who has a job in his gift. A touch of 'dropsy' makes the whole world kin. That this has long gone on is scarcely in doubt; how much of it goes on we are in no position to quantify; and inasmuch as it may be a basic feature of the culture of a particular area or of a particular trade, it is perhaps a mistake to call it 'exploitation'. To the unemployed individual affected by it, however, such friends and acquaintances appear to have power, and to know that they have it, and that he therefore has need of them.

All this probably does not apply nearly so much to the young unemployed, to school leavers and to those in their late teens and early twenties. Such evidence as there is suggests that unemployment may have rather less effect on friendship in this age range than among older unemployed (Carroll, 1979; Roberts, 1981). If *age* is indeed the relevant factor: it very probably is, but it may also even more reflect the difference between *generations*. We pointed out earlier that there is very little information about the young unemployed of the thirties, but what information we do have suggests that their situation was very different from that of the young unemployed of our time. In the thirties, for instance, age-related wage differentials favoured the young over the adult worker, whereas the relative erosion of age-related differentials nowadays favours the experienced worker, which makes it even harder for the inexperienced to get a start. Another way in which the generations may differ is in the significance to them of work as a source of *identity*. In the 1980s we are not only experiencing high levels of unemployment, but for a number of years there has also been much publicity, in a sense much education, devoted to the idea of change: society and the economy are changing, and will continue to change, and individuals must be ready to be flexible, prepared to retrain every so often, to have more than one 'career' – and so on. In effect the relatively high subjective probability of experiencing some unemployment, combined with the perceived ephemerality of any one occupation, may increasingly undermine the perceived relevance of work to one's personal identity. There are hints of this in the thirties. Some of Bakke's men, for instance, talked regretfully of 'good' youngsters no longer committing themselves to apprenticeships and a life-long trade (Bakke, 1933). In the 1980s, an almost obsessive preoccupation with the inevitability of change and the consequent need for flexibility, has made the very notion of a 'life-long' occupation an anachronism. This is, of course, another instance of the failure to distinguish between events at macro- and micro-levels of analysis, but that need not concern us here. The potentially very important social psychological consequence is the possible erosion of work as a significant source of identity, through the perceived temporary nature of occupations as well as through encounter with unemployment. If that happens, or inasmuch as it has happened, it will change expectations which people have about themselves and each other with respect to work. It will close the gap in status between those who have and those who do not have a job, because having or not having a job can then be acceptably modified by 'at this time' or 'for the time being'. The closing of that gap will significantly reduce many tensions of friendship, especially as perceived by the unemployed. There are no clear-cut data on this issue, and to clarify it will require data systematically collected over many years. Meanwhile it would be wise not to attribute automatically to age, a *developmental* factor, what in fact may be more validly explained in terms of generation or period, essentially *historical* factors.

The heightened sensitivity of the unemployed to loyalty, and especially to disloyalty, appears to be a very general effect of becoming unemployed. It is fundamentally a product of the unemployed individual's sense of his vulnerability. That also appears to be the most distinctive aspect of his view of employers and of the staffs of Benefit Offices. Once again there is little hard evidence: such as there is derives almost wholly from case-studies and autobiographical accounts; it is, however, consistent, and has been so since the thirties. Employers are seen as exploiting the weakness and insecurity of the unemployed worker, or at least as trying to exploit him: so they offer lesser jobs than he is qualified to do, for lower wages, and worse conditions. Very simply, the employers are seen as trying to force the unemployed to 'trade down', and there is some substance in this, especially in the case of 'older' workers (e.g. Bakke, 1933; Daniel, 1974a; Marsden and Duff, 1975; Daniel and Stilgoe, 1977; Sinfield, 1981; and, by implication, Dyer, 1973). The 'fault' may often lie with the overall economic situation rather than with the employer as a person, and a particular unemployed individual talking about a particular employer sometimes recognises this: but the unemployeds' *stereotype* of 'employers' is that of a class trying to take advantage of them, to exploit them. This belief is reinforced by the widespread tendency of employers to ignore written enquiries and even formal applications for jobs. Where this happens – and especially when it happens to the initially highly motivated unemployed individual who writes many letters – employers come to be seen as coldly, as it were degradingly, indifferent. Looked at objectively, firms inundated with letters and applications may simply not have the resources to acknowledge them all: from the standpoint of the unemployed, however, it underlines for him his powerlessness – and thereby his vulnerability to exploitation.

On Benefit Office staff, such comment as there is ranges mostly from the critical, through the hostile, to the openly angry (e.g. Bakke, 1933; Beales and Lambert, 1934; Gould and Kenyon, 1972; Marsden and Duff, 1975; the Schlackman Research Organisation Ltd, 1978). Since for various reasons this is understandable and to be expected, it should be said at the outset that there are also favourable and even sympathetic comments. To paraphrase, there is the 'they are no better than us' type of comment, followed by complaints of officiousness and downright nastiness; but there is also the 'they're just doing their job' comment followed by a psychological equivalent of shrugging of shoulders; and every so often there are hints of appreciation, especially of blind eyes turned to a little black economy (Marsden and Duff, 1975; Jenkins, 1978). It would be quite wrong to say that the unemployed almost universally see the staffs of Benefit Offices as looking down on claimants, or as positively enjoying and abusing their power. The *system*, however, and the *conditions* in which it operates, is perceived as a machine against which the unemployed individual is for all practical purposes powerless. He therefore generally feels that he is regarded simply as a 'case' to be processed: at best as a routine case, basically treated with indifference; at worst as suspect, and so having to disclose much of his most private life.

In essence, where the most distinctive effects of unemployment on friendship were to sensitise the unemployed individual to *loyalty*, in relation to employers and Benefit Office staff it sensitises him to their *power*. Though they may seem very different, they are merely two manifestations of the same underlying condition: the unemployed individual's heightened sense of dependence and therefore of vulnerability – psychological as well as economic.

Before we go further: 'heightened sensitivity' can easily be read as 'over-sensitive', from which it is only a small step to the loose use of 'paranoid'. By 'heightened sensitivity' we mean primarily 'heightened self-awareness', sometimes perhaps combined with a slightly lower threshold for detecting possible threat. The basic fact, however, is that the unemployed *are* more dependent and vulnerable than other sections of society: they are more exposed to criticism and loss of status in the family; to the fading and loss of at least some friendships; to being taken advantage of by employers; to the power of potentially capricious officialdom. Very real vulnerability and heightened sensitivity interact to reinforce each other: the unemployed have good rounds for being sensitive to aspects of life which other people can usually take for granted.

This heightened sensitivity affects not only the unemployed individual's perception of the particular people with whom he interacts, but also, inevitably, his perception of others in general, of 'society'. He knows that he belongs to – or rather, that he is *classified* as belonging to – a section of society which society as a whole regards as a 'problem': and that, as such, others at best see him as a victim of economic forces; or, more likely, as somehow vaguely inadequate; or, quite often, as just idle – a scrounger who could find work if he really wanted it, but prefers to live on benefit financed by others. To be unemployed is to see oneself as set apart, at best as an object of pity, at worst as a target for contempt: and that in turn has given rise to the concept of unemployment as *stigma*.

The literature on unemployment frequently cites examples of the unemployed individual's sense of stigma, and the stigma associated with unemployment has come to be regarded as one of its most damaging social and psychological consequences (e.g. Gould and Kenyon, 1972; Marsden and Duff, 1975; Harrison, 1976; Hayes and Nutman, 1981; Sinfield, 1981). We do not in any way wish to minimise the importance of this stigma, and the damage which it brings. Nevertheless, the use of the concept of 'stigma' in connection with unemployment requires rather more careful analysis than it has so far received. Here, too, as in the case of the Work Ethic with which it is closely linked, a concept has to quite an extent become a self-fulfilling prophecy; and in doing so it has probably aggravated a problem which was and is quite serious enough on its own.

There are, as it were, three parties to this issue: the unemployed individual who has, or may have, a sense of stigma; other people, and not least the media on behalf of 'society', who do the stigmatizing; and social scientists, who identify certain behaviours as indicative of stigma, whether as stigmatizing or as responses to stigma. Our first task is to try to identify the nature of the phenomenon with which we are concerned.

The term stigma, then, will be used to refer to an attribute [of a person] that is deeply discrediting, but it should be seen that a language of *relationships*, not attributes is really needed ... the central feature of the stigmatized individual's situation in life can now be stated. It is a question of what is often, if vaguely, called 'acceptance'. Those who have dealings with him fail to accord him the respect and regard which the non-contaminated aspects of his social identity have led them to anticipate extending, and have led him to anticipate receiving.

(Goffman, 1968, pp. 13 and 19. Our italics.)

Psychologically, stigmatization and a sense of stigma are both products of attribution and social comparison processes (Heider, 1958; Festinger, 1954). The stigmatiz*er* perceives the stigmatiz*ed* to have a certain characteristic which is discreditable: in itself; or in the causes to which it is attributed; or in its apparent implications; or in any combination of these. The characteristic being discreditable, the individual who has it is to that extent less of a person than other, 'normal', people. The central theme of scrounger-hounding, for example, is that the unemployed could find work, but are too idle or too inadequate to do so, and therefore sponge on the rest of ordinary working people. The stigmatized do not deny that they have the characteristic: they may seek to hide it, precisely to avoid the stigma, but they do not – and this is psychologically crucial – fundamentally dispute it. What they do dispute is the construction which the stigmatizers put on the characteristic, the denigrating causes to which they attribute it, the demeaning implications which they associate with it. To the stigmatized it is the stigmatizers who are the 'lesser' persons, in their ignorance, in their bigotry, in their stupidity, in their fears, and so on. Indeed, if one response to carrying a stigma is to seek to hide it, another sometimes is to proclaim it as a strength, as a special virtue, as a source of superiority: the coping strategies may be utterly different, but they arise from the same sense of stigma, and of being unjustly discriminated against on its account. Stigmatization and a sense of stigma provide a classic and sad instance of how the same 'fact' may have profoundly different meanings for different sets of people, and in doing so distort relationships.

In essence a stigma diminishes the individual who bears it. In the simplest and most frequent case, it turns an individual who would 'normally' be a social and moral equal into an inferior: and in all cases, the essential and distinctive function and effect of stigmata is to increase the difference in status between stigmatizers and stigmatized, to the detriment of the stigmatized. The practical manifestations of this are the denial to the stigmatized individual of his full rights as an otherwise 'normal' person, and his own strong sense that he is being denied these rights. The rights in question may be no more than the casual courtesies customarily observed between peers; they may be rights in law (including the right not to be singled out by law), the denial of which reduces the stigmatized to a second-class citizen; in the most extreme form, the denial may be that of the right to freedom and to live. Given this, to what extent, and in what ways, does unemployment constitute a stigma?

There can be no doubt at all that when an individual sees himself as 'unemployed' he also feels that he is 'different' from people who have jobs. That is quite clear from every account of the unemployed which we have ever come across. Nevertheless, one caution is necessary: there are a number of occupations in which periodic unemployment is a normal occupational hazard; the psychologically critical factor is that the individual *sees* himself as somehow significantly 'unemployed' by the criteria of his trade. Allowing for this, seeing oneself as 'unemployed', and feeling 'different' because of it, is even so not the same as seeing oneself and feeling 'stigmatized'. The two may go together, but they certainly do not do so necessarily: one may see oneself as 'different' without feeling 'stigmatized'; one may see oneself as 'stigmatized' without feeling 'different' – except for finding oneself stigmatized. (It is indeed probably this second situation which is psychologically most hurtful, precisely because the individual feels that he is *not* different.) A sense of being different and a sense of stigma are distinct phenomena, such that each is a sufficient but neither is a necessary or inevitable cause of the other. The distinction is directly relevant to assessing the evidence on the stigma of unemployment.

Research of the 1970s provides quite unambiguous evidence that the unemployed often, very often, have a sense of stigma. They talk of wondering what the neighbours think; of sitting on 'skid-row' at the club; of not wanting their children to be looked down upon for having free school meals; of dressing in ways characteristic of men in work, so as to feel like everyone else; of feeling like 'regular commuters' on their way to a training centre – and so on (Cohen, 1972; Gould and Kenyon, 1972; Marsden and Duff, 1975; Briar, 1977; Campling, 1978; Hill, 1978). In one form or another, accounts of the unemployed of the seventies show keen awareness of the *social* status, that is the low social status, of the unemployed. This awareness was probably mainly due to the 'scrounging controversy' of the period (Emmett, 1977; Deacon, 1978); but it was also reinforced by the sense of second-class citizenship induced by the conditions for receiving benefit, and by the language of unemployment.

There is much less evidence of a sense of the stigma of unemployment in the accounts of the 1930s. The unemployed certainly felt that they were 'different' – from people who had work, from how they had been and felt when they were in work themselves (Jahoda *et al.*, 1933/72; Bakke, 1933). They often also felt bitter about being unwanted, at being displaced (the men by women, as well as by machines); and some felt deeply their loss of independence (Pilgrim Trust, 1938). By the late thirties, however, Eisenberg and Lazarsfeld (1938) wrote of evidence of a decline even in the importance attached to independence: and, unless we have missed it on each of a number of readings, the word 'stigma' does not occur once in that most definitive review of the period. The closest that Eisenberg and Lazarsfeld come to this concept is 'loss of prestige', much as Komarovsky, a little later, wrote of 'loss of authority' (Komarovsky, 1940). Loss of prestige or of authority, however, are neither socially nor psychologically equivalent to stigma: the one refers to no more than a relative decline, the other is discreditable in itself. Significantly, there is evidence of stigma of a kind: it is the stigma of *poverty* and its consequences (not least on appearance), not the stigma of being unemployed (Zawadski and Lazarsfeld, 1935; Pilgrim Trust, 1938; Komarovsky, 1940).

There are two fundamental differences between the research of the 1930s and of the 1970s. First, as we stressed in the Introduction, and this cannot be stressed too strongly, reactions to unemployment are profoundly affected by the extent of unemployment, both in numbers and over time. The research of the *thirties* covers a period of very high unemployment, itself preceded by some ten years of high unemployment (and we remind the reader that relevant research did not even begin until the thirties). The *seventies* saw only the onset of a rise in unemployment, after two decades of historically quite exceptionally low unemployment. The second difference is in the realm of concepts. Neither the concept of the 'Protestant Work Ethic' nor, as we have just pointed out, the concept of 'stigma', feature as such in the literature of the 1930s, certainly not to any noticeable or significant extent. Weber (1905/1976, translated by Talcot Parsons, 1930) may not have wholly invented the Protestant Work Ethic, any more than Goffman invented stigma (1963): assumptions loosely related to a work ethic can be seen in the literature of the thirties, for instance in the report of the Pilgrim Trust (1938) and in the Eisenberg and Lazarsfeld review; and occasionally there are also remarks which *we*, nowadays, might treat as evidence of stigma. Fundamentally, however, the concept of the Protestant Work Ethic and the concept of stigma are both concepts of *our* time. Ours is also a time in which the media quickly pick up, simplify, and disseminate initially subtle and complex technical concepts. Vague notions of a 'work ethic' and of the 'stigma' of unemployment have thus become part of everyday language – and in doing so have themselves created expectations in terms of a work ethic, and of unemployment as a stigma. The diffusion of vague concepts then increases the range of phenomena which are perceived to exemplify them – which in its turn is taken as proof of the validity of the concepts. And so the unemployed themselves talk of the stigma of unemployment, its degradation (e.g. Gould and Kenyon, 1972; Hill, 1978).

One very important factor in this is the interaction of concepts with levels of unemployment. It is significant that the concepts of the work ethic and of unemployment as stigma were *not* part of the language of the thirties, not even of its academic language. They seem to have come to the fore in the sixties and early seventies, when unemployment was at first exceptionally low, and remained low by historic (and absolute) standards even when it began to rise. It is, we suggest, much more plausible to stigmatize the unemployed in an age of full employment than in times of widespread unemployment: it is also more plausible to see life in terms of a work ethic when expansion brings a growth in the number of jobs, than when technology (and not just economic recession) seems inexorably to erode them. Thus by 1981, Sinfield wonders, at least in passing, whether men have perhaps less sense of stigma in the context of large-scale redundancies.

It is not quite as simple as that. As Deacon (1976) has shown, there was scrounger-hounding of the unemployed (as distinct from the traditional stigmatization of *paupers*) in the 1920s. He also points out that the scrounging controversy of the mid-seventies came at a time when unemployment was relatively much higher than ten years earlier, when there had been no scrounger-hounding (Deacon, 1978). The explanation in this latter case, he believes, is that people in work see their living standards threatened by the cost of their contribution to supporting the unemployed. They may have seen their living standards similarly threatened in the 1920s when the whole notion, and the system, of non-contributory benefits was still very new ('non-contributory' benefits refers to benefits not directly related to the beneficiaries' own earlier contributions, but financed out of 'everybody's' contributions to a national fund). Scrounger-hounding – or stigmatization of the unemployed – may therefore be related to a *critical* level of unemployment. When unemployment is very low and everyone is doing nicely, the long-term unemployed are mostly treated sympathetically, as people who need to be helped, for whom there need to be special 'programmes'; and the frictionally unemployed are no problem in any case (there are no signs of stigma among the redundant of Wedderburn's study of 1964, who had scarcely any trouble finding other jobs). At the other extreme, when unemployment is high, when almost anyone can find himself without a job, and when there are few if any jobs to be had, stigmatization comes to lack credibility – it could happen to oneself or, say, to one in ten or more of one's constituents (and their families and friends), and so on. Somewhere in between, however, or perhaps in response to relatively rapid change, a perceived threat to one's own living standards, a touch of envy (especially among the lower-paid employed), anger, priggishness, and the like, are easily set off into scrounger-hounding.

It is during such critical periods that the unemployed are stigmatized as such – that is, for not working rather than as poor: it is then that they see others as stigmatizing them, and that they feel stigmatized. That, we suggest, was the situation in the late sixties and even more so for most of the seventies. It is the literature of that period which has particularly drawn attention to the stigmatizing of the unemployed and to their sense of stigma, and it did so quite validly, given the facts of its time. Furthermore, such stigmatization as there may be, at any time, will find many unemployed very receptive to it, despite themselves: for another factor is that the unemployed so often feel frustrated, dislike their way of life, and themselves for leading it. Disdaining their situation and themselves, the unemployed can easily see themselves being disdained. As we said when we began on this, we do not deny that the unemployed often have a sense of stigma; that they often see others as looking down on them. It is, however, equally important to recognise that this sense of unemployment as a stigma is essentially a contingent phenomenon. It does not arise primarily because to be unemployed is to infringe some fundamental and absolute standard, such as the work ethic: it is very largely a function of the level of unemployment at any given time, and with it, of the probability of being unemployed oneself; that affects the potential stigmatizers as much as those who potentially see themselves as stigmatized.

The underlying social psychological process in all this is identification with reference groups (Shibutani, 1955; Hyman and Singer, 1968). When unemployment is very low, those who are more than frictionally unemployed will indeed, in the vast majority of cases, be people with 'problems': people who in some fairly fundamental ways are inadequate or incapacitated, probably to be pitied rather than scorned. The ordinary unemployed worker, the individual who normally has a job, neither sees himself to belong to that category, nor is he seen to belong to it, even when he is briefly unemployed between jobs. In periods of very high unemployment, when almost anyone can become unemployed, 'The Unemployed' include people like oneself, whether or not one happens to be employed or unemployed at the time; it also includes people like one's family, one's friends, one's neighbours. Under these circumstances 'The Unemployed' are not an inherently and automatically a degrading reference group – even though there are of course very sound practical reasons for not wanting to belong to it. At what we have called the 'critical' level of unemployment, however, the situation is much more ambiguous. The general tone seems to be set by an image of 'the unemployed' based on the hard-core unemployed, the inadequate, the more or less unemployable. When *that* is the image the unemployed ordinary worker feels tainted by association; he believes that others associate him with these 'inadequates', as indeed they often do (see, for example, Gould and Kenyon, 1972; Marsden and Duff, 1975; Hill, 1978; and Deacon, 1978, on 'scroungers'). The problem may be especially acute during periods of rapid *upward* change in levels of unemployment, as during the 1970s. For some two decades it had been valid to assume that almost anyone who wanted a job, and was fit to hold it, could find one; to be unemployed therefore implied that the individual was physically or mentally inadequate; or, treating this as an alternative, pathologically idle. It took time for people to accept that these assumptions were no longer valid, and might not be valid for some time to come. Meanwhile the growth in the numbers of unemployed seemed a growth in the number of scroungers, encouraged by over-generous benefits, and to be discouraged by being exposed, disgraced, and punished: and the ordinary unemployed worker himself, puzzled and depressed by finding it so difficult to get work after years of 'full employment', fell to wondering whether perhaps there truly was something wrong with him.

It was a period understandably high in stigmatization of the unemployed – with the unemployed themselves often understandably bewildered, more than half ready to be stigmatized, and therefore expecting others to stigmatize them. This was, however, a time of transition, the evidence from which is not necessarily a good guide to what happens during periods of stable levels of unemployment, and perhaps especially during prolonged periods of high unemployment.

A high level of unemployment which extends over many years may largely eliminate the stigma, and sense of stigma, of being without a job. It does not make 'The Unemployed' a positive reference group, the kind of group to which one aspires to belong and of which one wants to remain a member if one does belong to it. This brings us to the unemployed individual's perception of other unemployed, and his attitudes and behaviour towards them. The phenomena have perplexed observers for a very long time. Eden (1797) noted how the poor often preferred to be worse off outside the workhouse, in order to avoid associating with those inside, and being associated with them. Bakke (1933) and the Pilgrim Trust (1938) report how the unemployed themselves inform on other unemployed who do odd jobs to earn a little money – or are merely believed to do so. Bakke adds that officials had remarked that they would not be able to enforce regulations without informants from amongst the unemployed themselves; and the Pilgrim Trust comment that unemployment had in this way eroded the traditional solidarity of even the staunchest working-class communities. Jahoda *et al.* (1933/72) recorded a similar increase in informing in Marienthal, and informing continues (Marsden and Duff, 1975; Deacon, 1978).

It is important not to exaggerate the significance of informing. It is the action of a minority, and it is perhaps more understandable in the case of the unemployed than in many other instances of disloyalty. Since the unemployed individual so often dislikes his way of life, and himself for leading it, he may have more need than many for social comparisons which enhance his self-esteem: and it may therefore sometimes be particularly salient to him to feel that he is better than others who are in the same position as himself. In this, at least, there is nothing unique about the unemployed: the various sciences, for instance, are all riddled with intellectual Pharisees who, looking at one another, 'Thank God that they are not as other men are' (Luke, 18:11). Nevertheless, informing is symptomatic, in an extreme form, of a basic pattern: the lack of a feeling of solidarity among the unemployed, the lack of a sense of bond between them. The principal consequence of this, which has repeatedly puzzled commentators (and at times frustrated them), is the negligible political activities of the unemployed as a group. Eisenberg and Lazarsfeld (1938) did speculate whether high levels of unemployment had contributed to the rise of fascism. Writing in the seventies, however, but much concerned with the thirties, Verba and Schlozman (1977) and Fraser (1980), were far more struck by the lack of radicalism (right or left) of the unemployed, by their essential submissiveness. Here, as they saw it, was a group of manifestly disadvantaged people, suffering very real hardship: and all they did, when they did exceptionally get together, was to present a 'Humble Petition' to Parliament, and to sing 'America' outside the Senate – and go home (Fraser, 1980).

Yet this is not nearly so odd when one considers the position of the unemployed in terms of reference group and social comparison theory. The first and important fact is that the unemployed individual *does* make new friendships among the unemployed: from amongst people in the dole queue, for example, or at employment agencies. The unemployed also talk of making friends with people from social classes and occupational groups whom they would probably not have encountered in 'normal' times; and 'first-timers' in the dole queue sometimes remark how these experiences have changed their views about 'The Unemployed' (Gould and Kenyon, 1972; Marsden and Duff, 1975; Briar, 1977). Any one *particular* unemployed individual is thus quite likely to form new friendships with *particular* fellow unemployeds. The crucial fact, however, is that he does *not* form such friendships *because* the other is unemployed – as he might because he is a fellow lorry-driver, or teacher, or bankrupt businessman; or even more likely, because he is a fellow angler, stamp-collector or Muggletonian. Unemployment may be the *circumstance* under which people meet; it is not itself the basis and reason for continuing friendship. (The small numbers who join and participate in one of the various associations of the unemployed are almost certainly only a partial exception to this: some of them are no doubt interested in unemployment as a general economic and political issue which encompasses more than their personal problems; for many, probably for most, these associations are simply sources of help in hopefully only passing difficulties.)

The unemployed thus constituted a virtually unique negative reference group: its members, almost to a man and woman, do not want to belong to it. There are, of course, other negative reference groups, for example disadvantaged and stigmatized ethnic and religious groups, which are also problematic for those who belong to them. Some members of such groups may try to deny or hide their membership; and in the case of religious groups the individual can in the last analysis abandon his faith and its community, though perhaps only at great and painful personal cost. The vast bulk of a disadvantaged minority, however, either cannot just cease to belong to it, or would not want to leave it even if they could. Their predominant strategy in their ambivalence is therefore to proclaim a proud cohesiveness and to demand, and work for, full equality with the functional 'majority'. In most minorities the deserter or apostate is an exception within a body bound by common heritage or beliefs: among the unemployed, the 'deserter', as it were, is the norm. Moreover, it is not only the unemployed individual himself who normally wants to leave the ranks of the unemployed; society imposes a duty on him to do all he can to do so.

Unemployment is in essence perceived as a transitory state, and 'The Unemployed' are a reference group of which the ordinary unemployed worker sees himself as an unwilling and essentially temporary member. This may vary a little in practice, when there are persistent high levels of unemployment in a particular locality or occupation – or age group. Under those conditions, being employed (or being repeatedly unemployed) may come to be seen as a long-term prospect, even possibly as a way of life (e.g. Bakke, 1933; Sinfield, 1968; Marsden and Duff, 1975; Sinfield, 1981). In such circumstances, however, identification is first and foremost with 'around here', or 'in my trade', not with 'The Unemployed'. The crucial fact is that unemployment does not provide the psychological basis for making 'The Unemployed' a group with which one identifies, even when the label fits, and when one uses it to describe oneself. Unlike work groups, the unemployed are not linked by a common task, even a disliked one. Unlike occupational groups the unemployed do not have identifiable common assumptions based on similar training and experience. Unlike people at work, they do not have a work-place where they meet and interact as a matter of course. They are not like hobbyists, linked by common interests. Except for the young, they lead very restricted social lives. Finally, as we stressed early on, one of the most fundamental problems of the unemployed individual is that, as 'unemployed', he is defined by what he is *not*, which tells very little about what he is. As far as the unemployed individual is concerned, therefore, 'The Unemployed' are a very mixed collection of people, of which he does not want to be a part; and such friends as he may have amongst them will also almost always not want to be a part of it. The unemployed are mostly not hostile to one another, despite the evidence of a modicum of informing: on the contrary, they are probably more inclined to be sympathetic to each other than indifferent. They do not, however, seem to have a sense of a positive bond: and when one looks at their general situation it is difficult to see how such a bond might arise.

We stressed at the beginning that the way in which the unemployed individual sees others is profoundly affected by how he believes they regard him. His beliefs concerning this are partly shaped by his direct contact with others, and partly, at the end of the twentieth century, by the media: by the way in which the media present him and his like, and by the attitudes towards 'The Unemployed' which they represent as the attitudes of others, of 'society'. This has inevitably and understandably given rise to stereotype images of 'The Unemployed' and to stereotype attitudes towards them. At the extremes we have the unemployed as 'scroungers', who must be made to work, and the unemployed as 'victims', who must be helped in every way and compensated for their undeserved suffering. In between there is ambivalence and confusion, which is probably the position of most people, including many of the unemployed themselves. Moreover, it does not help when psychologists, *and* other specialists, however well intentioned, reinforce stereotype thinking. Yet that is precisely what we do when we present some very broad and rough generalisations as if they were universal laws: so we have The Stages of Unemployment, Unemployment as Stigma, The Protestant Work Ethic as a source of Feelings of Guilt and Inadequacy – and so forth. None of these generalisations is wholly without foundation, but, as we hope we have shown, they also greatly over-simplify the situation. Perhaps the most fundamental fact is that 'The Unemployed' are not a group of people but essentially an *economic category*. In practice, but not necessarily, they are also an *administrative category*, because the great majority of the unemployed depend on others, and especially on the state, to support them. Again in practice, but not necessarily, belonging to this economic–administrative category *seems* to be correlated with certain social and psychological characteristics and consequences. However, for a variety of reasons, the *size* of this category changes, up and down, over time; with size it changes in *composition*; and with changes in size and composition go changes in many of its social and psychological characteristics and implications.

From that standpoint we still have remarkably little evidence on the effects of unemployment: we have some for a few of the worst years of the Depression of the thirties; we have some from the fifties and sixties when, with rare exceptions, there was so much work to be had that the search was almost wholly for the social and psychological *causes* of unemployment; and we have a very small number of studies from the seventies and early eighties, the years which have turned out to be the beginning of the current high levels of unemployment. These fluctuations in size over time took place against a background of more steady continuous change in material conditions and attitudes and values. We are *not* saying that there are *no* regular, or at least fairly predictable, psychological effects of unemployment. The problems of what to do with one's time, for example, seems to be very disturbing and demoralising for the great majority of unemployed, and very recalcitrant. So probably is the lack of a structure of work-based role relationships; and so, for many, may be the loss of important aspects of identity related to work.

Yet many unemployed people might not have any of these problems, or would have them only in much reduced form, if they were not also *poor* as well as unemployed: and *if*, somehow, they were of independent means, they would certainly avoid that deeply scarring sense of second-class citizenship which so defaces their lives at presence. We do not at this time have any clear basis on which we can make the crucially important distinction between the effects of unemployment and the effects of the poverty which almost invariably goes with it. We know a little about the psychological and social psychological consequences of unemployment, and we shall be able to contribute to an understanding of these problems and their solution as we gradually build up our body of knowledge. No one gains, however, when the sense of the urgency of the problem means that early findings are presented and treated as if they were established laws.

# Bibliography and citation index

The bibliography lists almost all the references which we encountered in our search. The exception is a number of studies which we judged to be too esoteric – for example, reports of training programmes for Indians in Northern Ohio. References cited in the text are marked with an *.

Index page references are in bold type.

Albee, G.* The Protestant Ethic, sex, and psychopathology. *American Psychologist*, vol. 32, pp. 150–61, 1977.   **101**

Albert, T.* A forgotten generation. *New Statesman*, p. 312, 10 March 1978.   **40**

Alfano, A.M.* A scale to measure attitudes toward working. *Journal of Vocational Behaviour*, vol. 3, no. 3, pp. 329–33, July 1973.   **22, 27, 36**

Allen, D.E. and Sandhu, H.S. A comparative study of delinquents and non delinquents: Family affect, religion and personal income. *Social Forces*, vol. 46, no. 2, pp. 263–9, 1967.

Allport, G.W.* *Personality*. New York: Holt, 1937.   **83**

Antebi, R.N.* State benefits as a cause of unwillingness to work. *British Journal of Psychiatry*, vol. 117, pp. 205–6, 1970.   **44**

Anthony, P.D.*The Ideology of Work*. London. Tavistock Publications, 1977.   **101**

Arendt, H.* *The Human Condition*. Chicago: Chicago University Press, 1958.

Atkinson, A.B. and Trinder, C.* Pride, charity and the history of 'take-up'. *New Society*, pp. 262–3, 13 August 1981.   **100**

Baker, K. The new unemployment. *The Spectator*, p. 234, 12 February 1972.

Bakke, E.W.* *The Unemployed Man*. London: Nisbet, 1933.   **1, 10, 19, 23, 25, 28, 29, 30, 33, 35–6, 38, 52, 53, 54, 57, 58, 62, 67, 69, 70, 72, 74, 75, 110, 111, 114, 115, 116, 117, 120, 124, 126**

Banks, M.H. and Jackson, P.R.* Unemployment and risk of minor psychiatric disorder in young people: cross-sectional and longitudinal evidence. *Psychological Medicine*, vol. 12, pp. 789–98, 1982.   **38**

Banks, M. and Warr, P.* *Work and Mental Health among Lesser Qualified School Leavers*. S.S.R.C. Final Report, 1980.   **29**

Barlow, M.L. Vocational education and the American work ethic. *American Vocational Journal*, vol. 48, pp. 1 & 27, January 1973.

Barnes, W.F.* Job search models, the duration of unemployment, and the asking wage – some empirical evidence. *Journal of Human Resources*, vol. 10, no. 2, pp. 230–40, Spring 1975.   **36, 37**

Bartlett, F.C.* *Remembering: a Study in Experimental and Social Psychology*. Cambridge University Press, 1932.   **44**

Beales, A.L. and Lambert, R.S.* *Memoirs of the Unemployed*. London: Gollancz, 1934. **19, 21, 23, 24, 25, 42, 67, 72, 111, 117**

Beatty, R.W. Training the hard core unemployed. An occupational study looking at variables related to unemployment. *Dissertation Abstracts International*, vol. 32 (2-B) pp, 1263–4, August 1971.

Beatty, R.W.* Supervisory behaviour related to job success of hard core unemployed over a 2 year period. *Journal of Applied Psychology*, vol. 59, no. 1, pp. 38–42, February 1974. **64, 83**

Beatty, R.W.* A two year study of hard core unemployed clerical workers: effects of scholastic achievement, clerical skill and self esteem on job success. *Personnel Psychology*, vol. 28, pp. 165–73, 1975. **39, 83**

Beatty, R.W. and Beatty, J.R.* Longitudinal study of absenteeism of hard core unemployed. *Psychological Reports*, vol. 36, no. 2, pp. 395–406, April 1975. **40, 83**

Beck, A. A 20 hour week. New Society, p. 493, 20 August 1974.

Becker, H.S. *Outsiders. Studies in the Sociology of Deviance*. New York: The Free Press, 1966.

Becker, J.* *'In Aid of the Unemployed'. Public Works and Work Relief*. Baltimore, MS.: Johns Hopkins Press, 1965. **39**

Beckerman, W. How sacred is full employment? *New Statesman*, p. 607, 1 November 1974.

Bem, D.J.* Self-perception: an alternative interpretation of dissonance phenomena. *Psychological Review*, vol. 74, pp. 183–200, 1967. **83**

Bem, D.J.* Self-perception theory. In L. Berkowitz, (ed.), *Advances in Experimental Social Psychology*, vol. 6, pp. 1–62, 1972. **48, 83**

Bennett, D.* The value of work in psychiatric rehabilitation. *Social Psychiatry*, vol. 5, no. 4, pp. 224–30, 1970.

Berger, P.L. *The Human Shape of Work*. Indiana: Gateway Editions Ltd/MacMillan, 1964.

Berger, P. and Luckmann, T.* *The Social Construction of Reality*. London: Allen Lane, 1967. **66**

Berthoud, R.* Unemployed professionals and executives. London: Policy Studies Institute, vol. XLV, no. 582, 1979. **25, 28, 31, 36**

Best, F. *The Future of Work*. New Jersey: Prentice-Hall, chapters 1, 2, 3, 4, 5, 8, 9, 14, 1973.

Beveridge, W.H.* *Unemployment – a Problem of Industry*, (1909). London: Longmans Green, 1931. **12, 13, 25, 30–31, 33, 34, 35, 36, 43, 44, 55, 91, 106, 108**

Beveridge, W.H. *Full Employment in a Free Society*. London: Allen and Unwin Ltd, 1944.

Blake, G.F., Mason, J., Hoffman, D.E. and Penn, L.* Recruiting unemployed youth as planners of youth employment. School of Urban Affairs, Portland State University, Oregon 97207, Series SSP, 0914, 1978. **39**

Bland, A.E., Brown, P.A. and Tawney, R.H.* (eds.). *English Economic History: Selected Documents*. London: Bell, 1914. **105, 107**

Bleasdale, A.* *Boys from the Black Stuff.* BBC T.V. Series. 1982. **112**

Blood, M.R.* Work Values and Job Satisfaction. *Journal of Applied Psychology,* vol. 53, no. 6, pp. 456–9, 1969. **101**

Bloomberg, C.M. Job training for dropouts. *American Journal of Orthopsychiatry,* vol. 37 (4), pp. 779–86, 1967.

Blumer, H.* Society as symbolic interaction (1962). Reprinted in J.G. Manis and B.N. Meltzer (eds.). *Symbolic Interaction: a Reader in Social Psychology,* pp. 97–108. Boston, Mass.: Allyn and Bacon, 1972. **96**

Boon, G.T.* *A Household Survey of Unemployment in Ashington and Bedlington.* Regional Studies, vol. 8, pp. 175–84. London: Pergamon Press, 1974. **13**

Bosanquet, N. and Standing, G.* Government and unemployment 1966–70. A study of policy and evidence. *British Journal of Industrial Relations,* vol. 10 (2) pp. 180–92, 1972. **13**

Bourne, R.* Trial by unemployment. *New Society,* p. 70, 14 July 1979. **39**

Bowser, S.E.* An action research approach to central city unemployment. *Journal of Vocational Behaviour,* vol. 4 (1), pp. 115–24, January 1974. **40**

Brenner, M.H.*Estimating the Social Costs of National Economic Policy: Implications for Mental and Physical Health and Criminal Aggression.* Joint Economic Committee of Congress, Paper no. 5, Washington D.C., U.S. Govt Printing Office, 1976. **74**

Brenner, M.H.* Economy and Mental Health. Material supplied by the Everyman Programme, Granada Television, Manchester, Spring, 1979.

Brewerton, D.S., and Nichols, P.J.R. Return to work. *British Medical Journal.* vol. 2, pp. 1006–7, 1977.

Briar, K.H.* The effect of long term unemployment on workers and their families. *Dissertation Abstract International,* vol. 37 (9–A), p. 6062, 1977. **2, 15, 23, 25, 28, 37, 40, 42, 51, 53, 57, 59, 61, 62, 65, 67, 68, 72, 73, 75, 78, 80, 83, 111, 114, 120, 124**

Brieland, D. Children and families: a forecast. *Social Work,* vol. 19 (5), pp. 568–79, September 1974.

Brightbill, C.K. and Mobley, T.A.* *Education for Leisure-Centred Living.* New York: John Wiley and Sons, 1977. **70**

Brown, R.* Work. In P. Abrams (ed.), *Work, Urbanism, and Inequality,* pp. 55–159. London: Weidenfeld and Nicholson, 1978. **43, 56**

Buckingham, W. The great employment controversy. *Annals of the American Academy of Political and Social Science,* vol. 340, pp. 46–52, March 1962.

Burghes, L.* Who are the unemployed? In Frank Field (ed.), *The Conscript Army,* pp. 13–27. London: Routledge and Kegan Paul, 1977. **34**

Burns, E. The determinants of policy. In J. Becker (ed.), *In Aid of the Unemployed.* Baltimore, MS.: Johns Hopkins Press, 1965.

Campling, J.* Centres for 'layabouts'. *New Society,* p. 146, 27 April 1978. **32, 40, 64, 75, 82, 83, 111, 120**

Cantril, A.H. and Cantril, S.D. Unemployment, government and the American people. A National Opinion Survey. Washington D.C.: Public Research, 1978.

Carroll, P.* The social and psychological effects of unemployment upon young people. A review of the literature. Pers. comm. Department of Employment sponsored research, September 1979.  **38, 55, 115**

Catalano, R. and Dooley, C.D. Economic predictors of depressed mood and stressful life events in a metropolitan community. *Journal of Health and Social Behaviour*, vol. 18, pp. 292–307, September 1977.

Chadwick, D.* *The Secularisation of the European Mind in the Nineteenth Century.* Cambridge University Press, 1975.  **103**

Churchill, R.S.* *Winston Churchill: Young Statesman, 1901–1914.* London: Heinemann, 1967.  **12**

Cobb, S.* Physiologic changes in men whose jobs were abolished. *Journal of Psychosomatic Research*, vol. 18, pp. 245–58, 1974.  **18, 22**

Cohen, A.K. *Deviance and Control.* New Jersey: Prentice-Hall Inc., 1966.

Cohen, G.* The voluntary unemployed. *New Statesman*, p. 41, 14 January 1972.  **32, 40, 111, 120**

Coleman, D.C.* Labour in the English economy of the 17th century. In E.M. Carus-Wilson (ed.), *Essays in Economic History*, vol. 2. London: Edward Arnold, 1966.  **103**

Colledge, M. and Bartholomew, R.* The long term unemployed: some new evidence. Manpower Intelligence and Planning Division, MSC, *Employment Gazette*, pp. 9–12, January 1980.  **34, 41**

Coussins, J.* (ed.). *Dear Ssac . . .* London: Child Poverty Action Group, 1980.  **87**

Dabelko, D.D.* Reference group theory, social comparison theory and the study of politics. *Journal of Social Psychology*, vol. 99, no. 2, pp. 283–8, August 1976.  **16**

Daniel, W.W. Redundant pay-offs. *New Society*, p. 188, 27 July 1972.  **44**

Daniel, W.W.* *A National Survey of the Unemployed.* P.E.P. *Broadsheet, vol. 40*, no. 546, October 1974a.  **10, 19, 23, 25, 27, 28, 29, 31, 33, 34, 35, 36, 61, 62, 63, 72, 75, 91, 92, 116**

Daniel, W.W.* The reality of unemployment. *New Society*, p. 726, 19 August 1974b.

Daniel, W.W.* *The unemployment flow: stage 1.* Interim Report. Policy Studies Institute. 1981.  **10, 35, 39, 91, 92**

Daniel, W.W. and Stilgoe, E.* Towards an American way of unemployment. *New Society*, p. 321, 12 February 1976.

Daniel, W.W. and Stilgoe, E.* *Where Are They Now? A Follow-up Study of the Unemployed.* P.E.P. Broadsheet, vol. 43, no. 572, October 1977.  **10, 19, 23, 25, 28, 33, 34, 35, 36, 38, 64, 116.**

Davies, R., Hamill, L., Moylan, S. and Smee, C.H.* Incomes in and out of work. *Department of Employment Gazette*, pp. 237–43, June 1982.  **61, 62, 63, 66**

Deacon, A.* *In Search of the Scrounger: the Administration of Unemployment Insurance in Britain, 1920–31.* London: Bell, 1976.  **97, 99**

Deacon, A.* The scrounging controversy: public attitudes towards the unemployed in contemporary Britain. *Social and Economic Administration*, vol. 12, pp. 120–35, 1978.  **95, 97–98, 99, 120, 121, 122, 123, 124**

*Department of Employment Gazette.* Characteristics of the unemployed: sample survey, June 1976, pp. 559–74, June 1977.  **41**

*Department of Employment Gazette.* Measures to alleviate unemployment in the medium term: work sharing (Great Britain), vol. 86, pp. 400–2, April 1978.

Di Marco, N. and Gustafson, D.P.* Attitudes of coworkers and management toward hard core employees. *Personnel Psychology*, vol. 28, no. 1, pp. 65–76, Spring 1975. **92**

Dipboye, R.* Alternative approaches to deindividuation. *Psychological Bulletin*, vol. 84, no. 6, pp. 1057–73 November 1977. **52**

Doeringer, P.B.* (ed.). *Programs to Employ the Disadvantaged.* New Jersey: Prentice-Hall Inc., 1969.

Doll, R.E., and Gunderson, E.K. *Hobby Interest and Leisure Activity Behaviour among Station Members in Antarctica.* Navy Medical Neuropsychiatric Research Unit, San Diego, California (253900). Report no. (NMNRU–69–34), September 1969.

Douglas, J.* The view from the local office. In J. Coussins (ed.), *Dear Ssac . . .* London: Child Poverty Action Group, 1980. **85, 100**

Douglas, J.D. (ed.). *Deviance and Respectability.* New York: Basic Books Inc., 1970.

Dubey, S.N. Powerlessness and orientations towards family and children: a study in deviance. *Indian Journal of Social Work*, vol. 32, no. 1, pp. 35–43, April 1971.

Duval, S. and Wicklund, R.A.* *A Theory of Objective Self-Awareness.* New York: Academic Press, 1972. **48**

Dyer, L.D.* Aging and work. *Industrial Gerontology*, no. 17, pp. 38–46, Spring 1973. **28, 36, 37, 73, 116**

Eden, D. Self-employed workers: a comparison group for occupational psychology. *Organisational Behaviour and Human Performance*, vol. 9, pp. 186–214, 1973.

Eden, Sir Frederic Morton.* *The State of the Poor.* 1795–7. Facsimile Edition. London: Frank Cass & Co., 1966. **99, 105–6, 124**

Eisenberg, P. and Lazarsfeld, P.F.* The psychological effects of unemployment. *Psychological Bulletin*, vol. 35, pp. 358–90, 1938. **2, 7, 10, 15, 16, 20, 21, 25, 47, 120, 121, 124**

Emmerich, W.* Family role concepts of children ages six to ten. *Child Development*, vol. 32, pp. 609–24, 1961. **84**

Emmett, T.* How we rob the jobless. *New Society*, p. 440, 1 August 1977. **99, 120**

Ensor, R.C.K.* *England, 1870–1914.* Oxford: Clarendon Press, 1936. **12**

Fagin, L.H.* Unemployment and family crisis. *New Universities Quarterly*, vol. 34, no. 1, Winter, 1979/80. **59, 60, 68, 74, 78, 80, 111**

Feldman, J.M.* Race, employment and the evaluation of work. *Journal of Applied Psychology*, vol. 58, no. 1, pp. 10–15, 1973a. **25, 61, 83**

Feldman, J.M.* Race, economic class, and perceived outcomes of work and unemployment. *Journal of Applied Psychology*, vol. 58, no. 1, pp. 16–22, 1973b. **61, 83**

Festinger, L. Informal social communication. *Psychological Review*, vol. 57, pp. 271–82, 1950.

Festinger, L.* A theory of social comparison processes. *Human Relations*, vol. 7, pp. 117–40, 1954. **44, 66, 97, 118**

Festinger, L. *et al.* * *Social Pressures in Informal Groups: A Study of a Housing Project.* New York: Harper, 1950.   **81**

Festinger, L.* *The Theory of Cognitive Dissonance.* Evanston, Illinois: Row, Peterson, 1957.   **83**

Field, F.* Four week murder. *New Society*, p. 19, 3 January 1974.   **32, 100**

Field, F.* Long term paupers. *New Society*, p. 21, 7 July 1977a.   **61, 99**

Field, F.* Making sense of the unemployment figures. In Frank Field (ed.), *The Conscript Army.* London: Routledge and Kegan Paul, 1977b.   **13, 61**

Fillenbaum, G.G. and Maddox, G.L. Work after retirement. An investigation into some psychologically relevant variables. *The Gerontologist*, vol. 14, pp. 418–24, 1974.

Fineman, S. A psychosocial model of stress and its application to managerial unemployment. *Human Relations*, vol. 32, no. 4, pp. 323–45, 1979.

Fisher, A.A. The problem of teenage unemployment. Available from: National Technical Information Service, Springfield, Vancouver 22151. 1973.

Flaim, P.O.*Discouraged workers and changes in unemployment. *Monthly Labour Review*, vol. 96 (3), pp. 8–16, March 1973.   **17, 41; 64**

Flude, R.A. Development of an occupational self-concept and commitment to an occupation in a group of skilled manual workers. *Sociological Review*, vol. 25, no. 1, pp. 41–9, 1977.

Form, W.H. and Geschwinder, J.A.* Social reference basis of job satisfaction: The case of manual workers. *American Sociological Review*, vol. 27, no. 2, pp. 228–37, April 1962.   **28**

Forrester, T.* Who exactly are the unemployed? *New Society*, pp. 54–7, 13 January 1977.   **13, 28**

Forrester, T.* Destined for the dole? *New Society*, p. 612, 16 April 1978a.   **39**

Forrester, T. Society with chips and without jobs. *New Society*, p. 387, 16 November 1978b.

Frank, W.H. The long-term unemployed. In J. Becker (ed.), *In Aid of the Unemployed*. Johns Hopkins Press, 1965.

Fraser, C.* The social psychology of unemployment. *Marienthal*, an extreme case. In Jeeves, M. (ed.), *Psychology Survey No. 3*, London: Allen and Unwin, 1980.   **125**

Fraser, R.* (ed.). *Work: Twenty Accounts.* Harmondsworth: Penguin Books in association with *New Left Review*, vol. 2, 1969.   **66**

Friedlander, F. and Greenberg, S.* Effect of job attitudes, training and organisation climate on performance of the hard core unemployed. *Journal of Applied Psychology*, vol. 55, no. 4, pp. 287–95, August 1971.   **40**

Furnham, A.* The Protestant Work Ethic and attitudes towards unemployment. *Journal of Occupational Psychology*, vol. 55, pp. 277–85, 1982.   **101**

Gallaway, L.E. and Dyckman, Z. The full employment – unemployment rate: 1953–1980. *Journal of Human Resources*, vol. 5, no. 4, pp. 487–510, February 1970

Gardell, B. Reactions at work and their influence on non-work activities: An analysis of a sociopolitical problem in affluent societies. *Human Relations*, vol. 29, no. 9, pp. 885–904, 1976.

Garraty, J.A.* *Unemployment in History. Economic Thought and Public Policy.* New York: Harper and Row, 1978. **1, 9, 11**

Gaskell, G. and Smith, P. Race and alienated youth: A conceptual and empirical enquiry. L.S.E. Mimeo, 1981.

Gershuny, I. and Pahl, R.E.* Britain in the decade of the three economies. *New Society*, p. 7, 3 January 1980. **26**

Gibbs, J.P. Crime, unemployment and status integration. *British Journal of Criminology*, vol. 6, no. 1, pp. 49–58, 1966.

Giddens, A.* see Weber, M., 1976. **100**

Gillman, H.J. Economic discrimination and unemployment. *American Economic Review*, vol. 55, pp. 1077–96, 1965.

Gilroy, C.L. Investment in human capital and black and white unemployment. *Monthly Labour Review*, vol. 98, no. 7, pp. 13–21, July 1975.

Ginzberg, E. 'The job problem'. *Scientific American*, pp. 43–51, November 1977.

Goffee, R.* When the pit closes. *New Society*, p. 134, 20 April 1978. **37**

Goffman, E.* *Stigma: Notes on the Management of Spoiled Identity.* Harmondsworth: Pelican Books, 1968. **118, 121**

Goffman, E.* *The Presentation of Self in Everyday Life.* Harmondsworth: Pelican Books, 1969a. **49**

Goffman, E.* *Asylums: Essays on the Social Situation of Mental Patients and Other Inmates.* Harmondsworth: Pelican Books, 1969b. **52**

Golding, P. and Middleton, S.* Why is the press so obsessed with welfare scroungers? *New Society*, pp. 195–97, October 1978. **99**

Goldstein, B. and Eichhorn, R.L.* The changing Protestant Ethic: rural patterns in health, work and leisure. *American Sociological Review*, vol. 26, no. 4, pp. 557–65, 1961. **101**

Goodchilds, J.D. and Smith, E.E.* The effects of unemployment as mediated by social status. *Sociometry*, vol. 26, no. 3, pp. 287–93, September 1963. **25, 37**

Goodman, P. and Salipante, P.* Hiring, training and retraining the hard core unemployed. *Journal of Applied Psychology*, vol. 58, no. 1, pp. 23–33, 1973. **15**

Goodman, P. and Salipante, P.* Organisational rewards and retention of the hard core unemployed. *Journal of Applied Psychology*, vol. 6, no. 1, pp. 12–21, February 1976. **83, 92**

Gore, S.* The effect of social support in moderating the health consequences of unemployment. *Journal of Health and Social Behaviour*, vol. 19, pp. 157–65, June 1978. **58, 96**

Gould, T. and Kenyon, J.* *Stories from the Dole Queue.* Published in association with *New Society*, London: Temple Smith, 1972. **23, 24, 42, 52, 53, 57, 65, 67, 72, 87, 111, 114, 117, 118, 120, 121, 123, 124**

Gouldner, A.W.* The norm of reciprocity: a preliminary statement. *American Sociological Review*, vol. 25, pp. 161–78, 1960. **53**

Greenberg, J.* Equity, equality and the Protestant Work Ethic: allocating rewards following fair and unfair competition. *Journal of Research in Personality*, vol. 13, pp. 81–90, 1978. **101**

Griew, S. *Job Re-design.* Paris: O.E.C.D., 1964.

Griffin, D. Youth unemployment; can vocational education do anything about it. *American Vocational Journal*, vol. 52, no. 7, pp. 24–5, October 1977.

Gross, N., McEachern, A.W. and Mason, W.* *Explorations in Role Analysis: Studies of the School Superintendancy*. New York: Wiley, 1958. **56**

Guthrie, H.W. The prospect of equality of incomes between white and black families under varying rates of unemployment. *Journal of Human Resources*, vol. 5, no. 4, pp. 431–46, February 1970.

Haber, W. and Kruger, D. The role of the United States Employment Service in a changing economy. *Studies in Employment and Unemployment*. Kalamazoo, Michigan: Upjohn, Institute for Employment Research, February 1964.

Haber, W. *et al.* The impact of technological change: the American experience. *Studies in Employment and Unemployment*. Kalamazoo, Michigan: Upjohn Institute for Employment Research, September 1963.

Hafeez, A. A study of ascendance – submission among engineering, humanities and science students, employed engineers, and supervisors. *Indian Journal of Social Work*, vol. 32, no. 1, pp. 95–8, April 1971.

Hallaire, J. *Part-time Employment*. Paris: O.E.C.D., 1968.

Handa, M.L. and Skolnik, M.L. Unemployment, expected returns and the demand for university education in Ontario: some empirical results. *Higher Education*, vol. 4, no. 1, pp. 27–45, February 1975.

Hannah, S. Causes of unemployment. In Frank Field (ed.), *The Conscript Army*, London: Routledge and Kegan Paul, 1977.

Harrison, B.H. Work and leisure in industrial society. *Past and Present*, pp. 96–102, April 1965.

Harrison, R.* The demoralising experience of prolonged unemployment. *Department of Employment Gazette*, pp. 339–48, April 1976. **21, 25, 37, 41, 72, 118**

Hartlage, L.C. and Johnson, R.P.* Developing work behaviour in the hard core unemployed with videoplayback. *Perceptual and Motor Skills*, vol. 33, no. 3, pt 2, 1343–6, December 1971. **75**

Hartley, J.F. Psychological approaches to unemployment. *Bulletin British Psychology Society*, vol. 33, pp. 412–14, 1980. **2**

Hawkins, K.* *Unemployment. Facts, Figures and Possible Solutions for Britain.* Harmondsworth: Pelican Books, 1979. **28, 62, 67, 91**

Hayes, J. and Nutman, P.* *Understanding the Unemployed; The Psychological Effects of Unemployment*. London: Tavistock, 1981. **20, 101, 118**

Heider, F. *The Psychology of Interpersonal Relations*. New York: Wiley, 1958. **83, 118**

Helson, H.* *Adaptation Level Theory*. New York: Wiley, 1964. **16, 46**

Hepworth, S.J. Moderating factors of the psychological impact of unemployment. MRC Social and Applied Psychology Unit. Sheffield University. Memo 321, May 1979.

Herron, F. *Labour Market in Crisis*. London: Macmillan, 1975.

Hershey, R.* Effects of anticipated job loss on employee behaviour. *Journal of Applied Psychology*, vol. 56, no. 3, pp. 273–5, 1972. **18, 46**

Hewitt, J.P.* *Self and Society: A Symbolic Interactionist Social Psychology*. Boston, Mass.: Allyn and Bacon, 1976. **49**

Hill, J.* The psychological impact of unemployment. *New Society*, pp. 118–20, 19 January 1978.   **21, 23, 24, 25, 38, 46, 51, 57, 60, 65, 68, 69, 74, 75, 111, 120, 121, 123**

Hill, M.J.* Are the workshy a myth? *New Society*, p. 191, 30 July 1970.   **34**

Hill, M. *et al.*\* *Men Out of Work*. Cambridge University Press, 1973.   **23, 34, 64**

Hobsbawm, E.J.* *Labouring Men: Studies in the History of Labour*. London: Weidenfeld and Nicolson, 1968.   **103**

Hodge, R.W.* Toward a theory of racial differences in employment. *Social Forces*, vol. 52, no. 1, pp. 16–31, September 1973.   **34**

Holland, S.S. Long term unemployment in the 1960s. *Monthly Labour Review*, vol. 88, no. 9, pp. 1069–75, 1965.

Hughes, J.* Employ the young. *New Society*, p. 74, 14 October 1976.   **38**

Hutson, R.H. and Smith, J.R.* A community wide approach to training the hard core. *Personnel Journal*, vol. 48, no. 6, pp. 428–33, 1969.   **11, 64**

Hyman, H.H. and Singer, E.* (eds.). *Readings in Reference Group Theory and Research*. London: Collier-Macmillan, 1968.   **123**

Ilfeld, F.W. Characteristics of current social stressors. *Psychological Reports*, vol. 39, pp. 1231–47, 1976.

Inglis, K.S.* *Churches and the Working Classes in Victorian England*. London: Routledge and Kegan Paul, 1964.   **103**

Jahoda, M.* The psychological meanings of unemployment. *New Society*, p. 492, 6 September 1979a.

Jahoda, M.* The impact of unemployment in the 1930s and 1970s. C.S. Myers Lecture, 1979b.   **2, 44, 55, 62**

Jahoda, M., Lazarsfeld, P.F. and Zeisel, H.* *Marienthal. The Sociography of an Unemployed Community* (1933). London: Tavistock, 1972.   **1, 9, 19, 20, 23, 25, 26, 37, 54, 55, 57, 59, 61, 62, 65, 68, 70, 73, 74, 75, 78, 120, 124**

James, W.* *The Principles of Psychology*. New York: Holt, 1890.   **77, 83**

Jenkins, C. and Sherman, B.* *The Leisure Shock*. London: Eyre Methuen, 1979. **70, 101**

Jenkins, R.* Doing a double. *New Society*, p. 121, 20 April 1978.   **26, 71, 117**

Jones, E.L.* Industrial capital and landed investment. In E.L. Jones and G.E. Mingay (eds.), *Land, Labour and Population in the Industrial Revolution*, pp. 47–71, London: Arnold, 1967.   **104**

Kaplan, H.R. and Tausky, C. Work and the welfare Cadillac: the function of and commitment to work among the hard core unemployed. *Social Problems*, vol. 19, no. 4, pp. 469–83, Spring 1972.

Kasl, S.V.* Work and mental health. In J. O'Toole (ed.), *Work and the Quality of Life*. Cambridge, Mass.: M.I.T. Press, pp. 171–96, 1975.   **58**

Kasl, S.V. and Cobb, S. Blood pressure changes in men undergoing job loss: a preliminary report. *Psychosomatic Medicine*, vol. 32, no. 1, pp. 19–37, 1970. **46**

Kasl, S.V., Gore, S. and Cobb, S.* The experience of losing a job: reported changes in health, symptoms and illness behaviour. *Psychosomatic Medicine*, vol. 37, no. 2, pp. 107–21, March/April 1975.   **18, 22, 42, 46, 58, 62, 74, 96**

Katz, A.* Schooling, age and length of unemployment. *Industrial Labour Relations Review*, vol. 27, no. 4, pp. 597–605, July 1974.   **34**

Katz, D. and Kahn, R.L.* *The Social Psychology of Organisations*, 2nd edn, New York: John Wiley and Sons, 1978. **55, 89**

Keating, P.* (ed.). *Into Unknown England, 1866–1933: Selections from the Social Explorers*. London: Fontana/Collins. 1976. **103**

Kelly, J.R. Leisure as compensation for work constraint. *Society and Leisure*, vol. 8, no. 3, pp. 73–82, 1976.

Kelvin, P.* A social psychological examination of privacy. *British Journal of Social & Clinical Psychology*, vol. 12, pp. 248–61, 1973. **53**

Kelvin, P.* *The Bases of Social Behaviour*. London: Holt, Rinehart and Winston, 1970. **33, 84**

Kelvin, P.* Social psychology 2001: the social psychological bases and implications of structural unemployment. In R. Gilmour and S. Duck (eds.), *The Development of Social Psychology*. London: Academic Press, 1980a. **46**

Kelvin, P. The frustrations of unemployment. *MIMS Magazine*, 15 May 1980b.

Kelvin, P. Work as a source of identity: the implications of unemployment. *British Journal of Guidance and Counselling*, vol. 9, pp. 2–11, 1981.

Kelvin, P. Work, unemployment and leisure: myths, hopes and realities. In *Work and Leisure: The Implications of Technological Change*. Leisure Studies, Association Conference Proceedings, no. 4. Edinburgh: TRRU, 1982.

Kelvin, P.* The historical dimension of social psychology: the case of unemployment. In H. Tajfel, (ed.), *The Social Dimension*, vol. 2, pp. 405–22 Cambridge University Press, 1984. **73, 99, 102, 103**

Killian, L.* The significance of multiple-group membership in disaster. *American Journal of Sociology*, vol. 57, pp. 309–14, 1952. **56**

Kinn, J.M. Unemployment and midcareer change: a blueprint for today and tomorrow. *Industrial Gerontology*, no. 17, pp. 47–59, Spring 1973.

Klein, V. *Women Workers*. Paris: O.E.C.D., 1965.

Komarovsky, M.* *The Unemployed Man and His Family*. New York: Octagon Books, 1940. **2, 9, 10, 23, 42, 53, 57, 59–61, 68, 69, 78, 79, 80, 111, 113, 114, 120**

Laman Trip, W.C.S. Werkgelegenheid voor de jeugel. *Mens en Ondemerring*, vol. 22, no. 2, pp. 80–9, 1968.

Lawlis, G.F. Motivational factors reflecting employment instability. *Journal of Social Psychology*, vol. 84, no. 2, pp. 215–23, August 1971.

Layard, R.* Have job centres increased long-term unemployment? Discussion paper No. 62 arising from S.S.R.C. Workshop on Unemployment, 5 November 1979. **32**

Lebbing, W. De social ongelijkheid tussen beambten en arbeiders in de ondemerning. *Mens en Ondemerring*, vol. 22, no. 2, pp. 71–9, 1968.

Lefcourt, H.M.* Locus of control. *Current Trends in Theory and Research*. New York: Lawrence Erlbaum Associates, 1976. **41, 112**

Lehrmann, E. Youth unemployment: vocational education as partner or reactor? *American Vocational Journal*, vol. 52, no. 9, pp. 30–33, December 1977.

Lerner, M.J., Miller, D.T. and Holmes, J.G.* Deserving and the emergence of forms of justice. In L. Berkowitz (ed.), *Advances in Experimental Social*

*Psychology*, vol. 9, pp. 133–62, London: Academic Press, 1976. **112**

Levison, A. Unemployment: the problem we can solve. *Public Affairs Pamphlet*, no. 534, Public Affairs Committee Inc., 381 Park Av. South, New York 10016, 1976.

Levitan, A. and Belous, S. Thank God its Thursday! Could shorter workweeks reduce unemployment? *Across the Broad*, vol. 14, pp. 28–31, March 1977.

Lilley, S. *Men, Machines and History*. London: Lawrence and Wishart, 1965.

Lipsky, M.* *Street Corner Bureaucracy*. New York: Russell Sage Foundation, 1981. **85, 87**

Little, C.B. Stress responses among unemployed technical professionals. *Dissertation Abstracts International*, vol. 34, 1-A, p. 429, July 1973.

Lovie, S. Applied psychology in the post-industrial society. *Bulletin British Psychology Society*, vol. 31, pp. 281–84, 1978.

McLean, A.* *Occupational Stress*. Springfield, Illinois: Thomas, 1974. **56**

Mack, J.* Youth out of work. *New Society*, p. 117, 21 April 1977. **38**

Malpass, R. and Symonds, J.D. Value preferences associated with social class, sex and race. *Journal of Cross Cultural Psychology*, vol. 5, no. 3, pp. 282–300, September 1974.

Manis, J.G. and Melzer, B.N.* (eds.). *Symbolic Interaction: a Reader in Social Psychology*, 3rd edn, Boston, Mass.: Allyn and Bacon, 1978. **49**

Marbach, G.* *Job Redesign for Older Workers*. Paris: O.E.C.D., 1968. **35, 72**

Marsden, D. and Duff, E.* *Workless*. Harmondsworth: Pelican Books, 1975. **10, 16, 23, 24, 25, 26, 28, 29, 30, 33, 36, 38, 42, 46, 52, 53, 54, 56, 57, 59, 60, 62, 65, 67, 68, 69, 70, 71, 72, 73, 75, 78, 80, 87, 91, 110, 111, 113, 114, 116, 117, 118, 120, 123, 124, 126**

Mead, G.* *Mind, Self, and Society*, C. Morris (ed.), Chicago: Chicago University Press, 1934. **49**

Mead, M. Work, leisure and creativity. *Daedalus*, vol. 89, no. 1, pp. 13-23, 1960.

Meissner, M. The long arm of the job: a study of work and leisure. *Industrial Relations*, vol. 10, no. 3, pp. 239–60, October 1971.

Melching, D. and Broberg, M.* A national sabbatical system: implications for the aged. *Gerontologist*, vol. 14, no. 2, pp. 175–81, April 1974. **70**

Melvyn, P.* Youth unemployment in industrial market economy countries. *International Labour Review*, vol. 116, no. 1. pp. 23–38, July and August 1977. **38**

Merrens, M. and Garrett, J.* The Protestant Ethic scale as a predictor of repetitive work performance. *Journal Applied Psychology*, vol. 60, pp. 125–7, 1975.

Merton, R.K. *Social Theory and Social Structure*. New York: The Free Press, enlarged edn, 1968.

Mickens, A.I. Comment: unemployment theories and disadvantaged workers. *Society*, vol. 12, no. 3, pp. 22–5, March–April 1975.

Milham, S., Bullock, R. and Hosie, K.* Juvenile unemployment: a concept due for recycling? *Journal of Adolescence*, vol. 1, pp. 11–24, 1978. **55**

Miller, G.A., Galanter, E. and Pribram, K.H.* *Plans and the Structure of Behaviour*. New York: Holt Rinehart and Winston, 1960. **44**

Mirels, H. and Garrett, J.* The Protestant Ethic as a personality variable. *Journal of Consulting and Clinical Psychology*, vol. 36, pp. 40–4, 1971. **101**

Mitchell, B.R.* *European Historical Statistics: 1750–1970*. London: Macmillan, 1975. **14, 16**

Moore, P.* Counter-culture in a social security office. *New Society*, pp. 68–9, 10 July 1980. **85, 86, 87, 88, 89**

Moore, P.* Scroungermania again at the DHSS. *New Society*, pp. 138–9, 22 January 1981.

Morgan, B., Blonsky, M.R. and Rosen, H.* Employee attitudes towards a hard core hiring program. *Journal of Applied Psychology*, vol. 54, no. 6, pp. 473–8, December 1970. **64**

Morgan Guaranty Survey. *Spreading the Work*. New York: Morgan Guaranty Trust Co., February 1977.

Morgan Guaranty Survey. G.H. Moore, *Todays 'Full Employment'*. New York: Morgan Guaranty Trust Co., January 1978.

Morgan, H., Burns-Cox, J.J., Pocock, H. and Pottle, S. Deliberate self-harm: clinical and socio-economic characteristics of 368 patients. *British Journal of Psychiatry*, vol. 127, pp. 564–74, 1975.

Morgan, M.B. The effect of manpower development training program on attitude changes toward work and self concept. *Dissertation Abstracts International*, vol. 34, no. 6-A, p. 3150, December 1973.

Morse, N.C. and Weiss, S. The function and meaning of work and the job. *American Sociological Review*, vol. 20, pp. 191–8, 1955.

Mukherjee, S. *Unemployment Costs*. P.E.P. Broadsheet, vol. 42, no. 561, February 1976.

Mukherjee, S. *Governments of Labour Markets: Aspects of Policies in Britain, France, Germany, Netherlands and Italy*. P.E.P. Broadsheet, vol. 42, no. 566, November 1976.

Murray, P.* The jobloss youth trap. *New Statesman*, p. 538, 22 October 1976. **40**

Napier, T.L., Maurer, R.C. and Bryant, E. The relevance of a human resources development model for understanding unemployment status within S.E. Ohio, Unpublished paper. Dept. of Agricultural Economics and Rural Sociology, The Ohio Agricultural Research and Development Organisation, Ohio State University. April 1978.

Napier, T.L., Maurer, R.C. and Bryant, B.G. Factors affecting unemployment status among residents of a lesser developed region of Ohio. Unpublished paper. Ohio State University, Columbus 43210 and University of Kentucky, Lexington 40506. Senes: Rss 1978 0957, October 1978.

Neulinger, J. Into leisure with dignity: social and psychological problems of leisure. *Society and Leisure*, vol. 6, no. 3, pp. 133–7, 1974.

*New Society*.* Special Report. Is youth unemployment really a problem? *New Society*, p. 287, 10 November 1977. **36, 38**

*New Society*. A doleful tale, vol. 52, no. 913, pp. 3–4, 3 April 1980.

Nicholls, Sir George.* *A History of the English Poor Law* (1854). New edn. edited by Willink, reprinted London: Frank Cass and Co. 3 vols, 1966. **99**

Niemi, B. The female–male differential in unemployment rates. *Industrial and Labour Relations Review*, vol. 27, no. 3, pp. 331–50, April 1974.

Noyce, R.N. Microelectronics. *Scientific American*, vol. 237, no. 3, pp. 63–9. September 1977.

O'Connell, A.N. The relationship between life style and identity synthesis and resynthesis in traditional, neotraditional and nontraditional women. *Journal of Personality*, vol. 44, no. 4, pp. 675–88, December 1976.

O'Connor, R.D. and Rappaport, J. Application of social learning principles to the training of ghetto blacks. *American Psychologist*, vol. 25, no. 7, pp. 659–61, July 1970.

O.E.C.D. Social Affairs Division. *Promoting the Placement of Older Workers*. Paris: O.E.C.D., 1967.

Oeser, O.A.* Methods and assumptions of fieldwork in social psychology. *British Journal of Psychology*, vol. 27, pp. 243–63, 1937. **60**

Ogren, E.H.* Public opinion about public welfare. *Social Work*, vol. 18, pp. 101–7, 1973. **95**

Ohashi, H.* Re-socialisation under the industrial change – social psychological research on unemployed miners, pt 1, *Tohoku Psychologica Folia*, vol. 33, no. 4, pp. 13–19, 1975a. **23, 25, 35, 42, 78**

Ohashi, H.* Re-socialisation under the industrial change – social psychological research on unemployed miners, pt 2, *Tohoku Psychologica Folia*, vol. 34, no. 1–4, pp. 124–31, 1975b. **23, 25, 30, 35, 42, 78**

O'Leary, V.* The Hawthorne effect in reverse: trainee orientation for the hard core unemployed woman. *Journal of Applied Psychology*, vol. 56, no. 6, pp. 491–4, 1972. **42, 64, 65, 83**

Opie, Roger. Sir Keith's dole queue. *New Statesman*, p. 337, 13 September 1974.

Osgood, M.H.* Rural and urban attitudes toward welfare. *Social Work*, vol. 22, no. 1, pp. 41–7, January 1977. **59, 95, 96**

Page, B. The crack-up of the unemployment machine. *New Statesman*, p. 460, 7 April 1978.

Pahl, R.E. Living without a job: how school leavers see the future. *New Society*, p. 259, 2 November 1978. **38**

Pahl, R.E. and Wallace, C.* 17–19 and unemployed on the Isle of Sheppey. Mimeo, 1980. **55**

Palmer, D. and Gleave, D. Moving to find work. *New Society*, p. 454, 31 August 1976.

Parker, S.* *The Future of Work and Leisure*. London: MacGibbon and Kee, 1971. **70**

Parker, S. The sociology of leisure: progress and problems. *British Journal of Sociology*, vol. 26, no. 1, pp. 91–101, March 1975.

Parkes, C.M.* *Bereavement: Studies of Grief in Adult Life*. Harmondsworth: Penguin Books, 1975. **114**

Parsons, T. *Action Theory and the Human Condition*. New York: The Free Press, 1978.

Patchen, M.* The effects of reference group standards on job satisfactions. *Human Relations*, vol. 11, no. 4, pp. 303–14, 1961. **97**

Paterson and Dayly.* *Men, Women and Jobs*. University of Minneapolis Press, 1936. **34**

Pearson, L.F.* Non work time: a review of the literature. Centre for Urban and

Regional Studies, University of Birmingham, Research Memorandum, 1965.

Peterson, E. Working women. *Daedalus*, vol. 93, pp. 671–99, 1964.

Pilgrim Trust.* *Men without Work*. Cambridge University Press, 1938.   **19, 23, 25, 26, 34, 37, 38, 44, 52, 54, 55, 58, 60, 62, 65, 66, 68, 70, 74, 75, 79, 120, 121, 124**

Powell, D.H.* The effects of job strategy seminars upon unemployed engineers and scientists. *Journal of Social Psychology*, vol. 91, no. 1, pp. 165–6, October 1973.   **40**

Rapoport, R. and Rapoport, R. *Leisure and the Family Life Cycle*. London: Routledge and Kegan Paul, 1975.

Rayman, R.A. *Price Stability and Full Employment: a Neo-Keynesian Policy for Growth without Inflation*. P.E.P. Broadsheet, vol. 41, no. 558, October 1975.

Reich, S. and Geller, A. Self image of social workers. *Psychological Reports*, vol. 39, pp. 657–8, 1976.

Richardson, H.W. and West, E.G. Must we always take work to the workers. *Lloyds Bank Review*, January 1964.

Richmond, G. Employment or development: public and private responses to youth unemployment. *American Vocational Journal*, vol. 53, no. 3, pp. 36–8, March 1978.

Ritti, R.R. Underemployment of engineers. *Industrial Relations*, vol. 9, no. 4, pp. 437–52, 1970.

Roberts, K.* *Leisure*. London: Longman, 1981.   **70, 115**

Rock, P. and McIntosh, M. *Deviance and Social Control*. London: Tavistock Publications, 1974.

Rockefeller Foundation, N.Y. Youth unemployment. Publication Office, the Rockefeller Foundation, 1133 Avenue of the Americas, N.Y. 10036, September 1977.

Rolt, P. Rehabilitation and the question of work. From psychiatric day care, which direction? Unpublished Social Work M.A. Thesis.

Rosen, H. and Turner, J. Effectiveness of 2 orientation approaches in hard core unemployed turnover and absenteeism. *Journal of Applied Psychology*, vol. 55, no. 4, pp. 296–301, August 1971.

Rosenblum, M. Discouraged workers and unemployment. *Monthly Labour Review*, vol. 97, no. 9, pp. 28–30, September 1974.

Rosenquist, B.A.* The impact of company training program on reducing the alienation of the hard core unemployed. *Dissertation Abstracts International*, vol. 32, no. 11-A, p. 6309, 1972.   **64**

Rotter, J.B.* Generalised expectancies for internal versus external control of reinforcement. *Psychological Monographs*, vol. 80, no. 609, 1966.   **41, 112**

Roy, D.F. 'Banana Time': Job satisfaction and informal interaction. *Human Organisation*, vol. 18, no. 4, pp. 158–68, 1959.

Royston Pyke, E.* *Human Documents of the Victorian Golden Age*, London: Allen and Unwin, 1967.   **103**

Saad, E.S. and Madden, J.S. Certified incapacity and unemployment in alcoholics. *British Journal of Psychiatry*, vol. 128, pp. 340–5, April 1976.

Salipante, P. and Goodman, P.* Training, counselling and retention of the hard core unemployed. *Journal of Applied Psychology*, vol. 61, no. 1, pp. 1–11, February 1976. **83**

Sartin, R.* Youth unemployment: part problem, part symptom. *American Vocational Journal*, vol. 52, no. 7, pp. 26–30, October 1977. **38**

Schervish, P.G. The structure of employment and the structure of unemployment. Unpublished paper. University of Wisconsin, Madison 53706, Senos: ASA 1978 2785, December 1978.

Schlackman Research Organisation.* Public attitudes towards the supplementary benefit system. Central Office of Information, 1978. **52, 53, 60, 94–95, 111, 114, 117**

Schlozman, K.L. and Verba, S. The new unemployment: does it hurt? *Public Policy*, vol. 26, no. 3, pp. 333–58, Summer 1978.

Schweitzer, N. N. The persistence of the discouraged worker effect. *Industrial and Labour Relations Review*, vol. 27, no. 2, pp. 249–60, January 1974.

Schwitzer, S.O.H.* The relative importance of personal factors affecting re-employment. *Dissertation Abstracts International*, vol. 27, no. 12-A, p. 3993, 1967. **41**

Scott, J.D. and Phelan, J.G. Expectancies of unemployed males regarding source of control of reinforcement. *Psychological Reports*, vol. 25, no. 3, pp. 911–3, 1969.

Seabrook, J. *What Went Wrong?* London: Victor Gollancz, 1978.

Seales, D.J. and Braucht, G.N. Work values of the chronically unemployed. *Journal of Applied Psychology*, vol. 59, no. 1, pp. 93–5, February 1974.

Seear, B.N. *Re-entry of Women to the Labour Market after an Interruption in Employment*. Paris: O.E.C.D., 1971.

Seiden, A.* Overview – research on psychology of women. *American Journal of Psychiatry*, vol. 133, no. 10, pp. 1111–23, 1976. **65, 68**

Seligman, M.E.P.* *Helplessness: On Depression, Development and Death*. San Francisco: Freeman, 1975. **41**

Shanthamni, V.S. and Hafeez, A. Some personality variables among engineering students and employed engineers. *Indian Journal of Social Work*, vol. 33, no. 4, pp. 323–30, January 1973.

Shaw, B.* *Major Barbara* (1905), pp. 72–3, Harmondsworth: Penguin Books, 1944. **34**

Sheppard, H.L. and Belitsky, A.M. Promoting job finding success for the unemployed. Upjohn Institute for Employment Research, Kalamazoo, Michigan, 1968.

Sherif, C.V., Sherif, M. and Nebergall, R.E.* *Attitude and Attitude Change: the Social Judgement Approach*. Philadelphia: Saunders, 1965. **46**

Sherif, M. and Hovland, C.V.* *Social Judgement*. New Haven, Conn., Yale University Press, 1961. **46, 73**

Shibutani, T.* Reference group perspectives. *American Journal of Sociology*, vol. 60, pp. 562–9, 1955. **123**

Shiskin, J. Employment and unemployment: the doughnut or the hole. *Monthly Labour Review*, vol. 99, no. 2, pp. 3–10, February 1976.

Showler, B.* Who are the unemployed? *New Society*, p. 146, 23 July 1979b.   **28, 30**

Showler, B.* Are the workshy a myth? *New Society*, p. 191, 30 July 1979.   **9**

Simon, Y.R.M. *Work, Society and Culture*. New York: Fordham University Press, 1971.

Sinfield, A. *The Long Term Unemployed* Paris. O.E.C.D., 1968.

Sinfield, A.* Poor and out of work in Shields: a summary report. In P. Townsend (ed.), *The Concept of Poverty,*, H.E.B. Paperback, 1974.   **21, 28, 41, 54**

Sinfield, A.* The blunt facts about unemployment. *New Universities Quarterly*, vol. 34, no. 1, Winter 1979/80.   **25, 33**

Sinfield, A.* *What Unemployment Means*. Oxford: Robertson, 1981.   **11, 13, 25, 28, 30, 33, 36, 38, 44, 63, 65, 78, 87, 88, 91, 113, 116, 118, 121, 126.**

Singell, L.D. Economic opportunity and juvenile delinquency: a case study of the Detroit juvenile labour market. *Dissertation Abstracts International*, vol. 30, no. 1-A, pp. 38–9, 1969.

Slater, R. Findings. Who goes first? *New Society*, p. 250, 6 August 1970.

Sleigh, J., Boatwright, B., Irwin, P. and Stanyon, R. How real is the threat of technological unemployment? Micro-Electronic Study Group. *Department of Employment Gazette*, pp. 115–21. February 1980.

Smee, C.H. Unemployment and poverty: some comparisons with Canada and the USA. Paper presented at S.S.R.C. workshop on Employment and Unemployment, Department of Employment, June 1980.

Solie, R.J.* Employment effects of retraining the unemployed. *Industrial and Labour Relations Review*, vol. 21, pp. 210–25, 1968.   **33**

Spreitzer, E. and Snyder, E.E.* Age, education and occupation as correlates of the meaning of leisure. *Psychological Reports*, vol. 35, pp. 1105–6, 1974.   **70**

Stevenson, O.* *Claimant or Client*. London: Allen and Unwin, 1973.   **87, 89**

Stone, E.* Job scope, job satisfaction, and the Protestant Ethic: a study of enlisted men in the United States Navy. *Journal of Vocational Behaviour*, vol. 7, pp. 215–24, 1975.   **101**

Stub, H.R.* The occupational characteristics of migrants to Duluth: a retest of Rose's hypothesis. *American Sociological Review*, vol. 27, pp. 87–8, 1962.   **30, 36**

Sturrock, J. Out of work, short of hope. *Newsweek*, p. 37, 13 March 1980.

Swinburn, P.* The psychological impact of unemployment on managers and professional staff. *Journal of Occupational Psychology*, vol. 54, pp. 47–65, 1981.   **2, 29, 36, 46, 51, 56, 61, 62, 63, 67, 68, 72, 80, 110**

Talbot, M. Women and leisure. Review for the Joint SSRC/Sports Council Panel on Leisure and Recreation Research, 1979.

Tausky, C. and Piedmont, E.B. The meaning of work and unemployment: implications for mental health. *International Journal of Social Psychiatry*, vol. 14, no. 1, pp. 44–9, 1967/68.

Tawny, R.H. (ed.) and Power, E.E. *Tudor Economic Documents: Being Select Documents Illustrating the Economic and Social History of Tudor England*. University of London Historical Series, no. 4, 3 vols., London 1924.

Taylor, A.J.P.* *English History 1914–1945*, Oxford: Clarendon Press, 1965.   **14**

Taylor, R. Work sharing and worklessness. *New Society*, p. 452, 23 November 1978.

Taylor, S.E. and Crocker, J.* Schematic bases of social information processing. In T.E. Higgins, Herman, C.P., and Zanna, M.P. (eds.), *Social Cognition: the Ontario Symposium*. vol. 1, pp. 89–134, New Jersey: Erlbaum, 1981. **44**

Taylor, K.F., Kelso, G.I. and Remenyi, A.G.* Psychological perspectives on the work of the Commonwealth Employment Service. *Australian Psychologist*, vol. 12, no. 3, pp. 273–83, November 1977. **40**

Thomas, K. Work and leisure in pre-industrial society. *Past and Present*, vol. 29, pp. 50–66, December 1964.

Toppen, J.T. Underemployment: economic or psychological. *Psychological Reports*, vol. 28, no. 1, pp. 111–22, February 1971.

Townsend, P.* The neglect of mass unemployment. *New Statesman*, p. 463, 7 October 1974. **61**

Triandis, H.C., Feldman, J.M., Weldon, D.E. and Harvey, W.M.* Designing pre-employment training for the hard to employ: a cross cultural psychological approach. *Journal of Applied Psychology*, vol. 59, no. 6, pp. 687–93, 1974. **42, 64**

Triandis, H.C., Feldman, J.M., Weldon, D.E. and Harvey, W.M.* Ecosystem distrust and the hard to employ. *Journal of Applied Psychology*, vol. 60, no. 1, pp. 44–56, 1975. **8, 15, 25, 40, 61, 83**

T.U.C. Reports. *Employment and Technology*, 1979.

*Statement on Sport and Recreation*, 20 May 1980.

U.S. Government Papers. *Policy Options for the Teenage Unemployment Problem.* Background paper, no. 13. Congress of the United States, Congressional Budget Office, Washington, D.C., 21 September 1976.

*How the Government Measures Unemployment.* United States Department of Labor Bureau of Labor Statistics, Report no. 505, 1977.

*Employment and Unemployment during 1978: An Analysis.*, United States Department of Labor Bureau of Labor Statistics. Special Labor Force Report 218.

*Employment and Earnings.* United States Department of Labor Bureau of Labor Statistics, vol. 26, no. 6, June 1979.

*Publications of the Bureau of Labor Statistics, January to June 1978.* United States Department of Labor Bureau of Labor Statistics, Report no. 564, 1979.

*State Profile of Unemployment and Employment, 1977.* United States Department of Labor Bureau of Labor Statistics, Report no. 539, 1978.

*Addressing Continuing High Levels of Unemployment.* An Interim Report to the President and the Congress of the National Commission for Manpower Policy. Report no. 4, April 1976.

*Public Service Employment and Other Responses to Continuing Unemployment.* An Interim Report to the Congress of the National Commission for Manpower Policy. Report no. 2, June 1975.

Van der does de Willebois. Een industrieel atelier voor part time werkende gehuwde vrouwen. *Mens en Ondemerring*, vol. 22, pp. 129–47, 1968.

University of Pittsburgh. The four-day workweek: fad or future. Proceedings of a conference conducted by the Graduate School of Business, University of Pittsburgh, 1973.

Van Wezel, J.A.M.* Herintreding in het arbeidsproces-cen onderzoek onder werklozen. *Mens en Ondemerring*, vol. 27, pp. 3–29, 1973. **34, 35**

Verba, S. and Schlozman, K.L. Unemployment, class consciousness and radical politics. What didn't happen in the '30s'. *Journal of Politics*, vol. 39, no. 2, pp. 291–323, May 1977. **125**

Ward, C. Significant living without paid employment. I.C.O. Conference – Significant Living without Work, 20 January 1980.

Warr, P. Psychological aspects of employment and unemployment. *Psychological Medicine*, vol. 12, pp. 7–11, 1982.

Watts, A.G. A policy for youth. *The Ditchley Journal*, vol. 4, no. 1, Whole edn, Spring 1977.

Watts, A. Preparing for life without work. Unpublished paper from National Institute for Careers Education and Counselling, Cambridge. NICEC Occasional Paper no. 1. Presented at I.C.O. Conference entitled 'Significant Living without Work', Durham University, 17–20 January 1980.

Webber, D. Social democracy as the midwife of change: a comparative survey of active manpower policy innovation in Sweden, Britain, and West Germany. Department of Government, University of Essex. For S.S.R.C. workshop.

Weber, M.* *The Protestant Ethic and the Spirit of Capitalism* (1904/5). New introduction by A. Giddens. London: Allen and Unwin, 1976. **53, 100–101, 102, 121**

Wedderburn, D.* *White Collar Redundancy*. University of Cambridge, Department of Applied Economics Occasional Papers no. 1, 1964. **2, 15, 18, 23, 28, 29, 34, 36, 46, 51, 56, 62, 72, 122**

Wedderburn, D.* Unemployment in the Seventies. *The Listener*, vol. 86, no. 2211, p. 193, 12 August 1971.

Weightman, G. Under the grill. *New Society*, pp. 5–7, January 1978. **87**

Wernimont, P.F. and Fitzpatrick, S. The meaning of money. *Journal of Applied Psychology*, vol. 56, no. 3, pp. 218–26, June 1972.

Wicklund, R.A.* Objective self-awareness. In L. Berkowitz (ed.), *Advances in Experimental Social Psychology*, vol. 8, pp. 233–77, London: Academic Press, 1975, **48**

Wicklund, R.A. and Frey, D.* Self-awareness theory: when the self makes a difference. In D.M. Wenger and R.R. Wallacher (eds.), *The Self in Social Psychology*, New York: Oxford U.P., 1980. **48**

Wiener, R.S. Consequences of a self-survey by a Belfast community. *Journal of Social Psychology*, vol. 93, no. 2, pp. 197–201, August 1974.

Wilkins, A. Latent talents. *Do-it-Yourself*, vol. 22, no. 10, October 1978.

Wilcock and Franke,* Unwanted Workers. Institute of Labour and Industrial Relations, University of Illinois, 1963. **41**

Wilensky, H.L. The uneven distribution of leisure: the impact of economic growth on 'free time' time. In O.E. Smigel (ed.), *Work and Leisure: A Contemporary Social Problem*. New Haven, Conn.: College and University Press.

Williamson, J.B.* Beliefs about the motivation of the poor and attitudes toward poverty policy. *Social Problems*, vol. 21, pp. 634–48, 1974.   **59, 95**

Wilson, J.M. Keeping the unemployed employed. *New Statesman*, pp. 147–8, 7 August 1970.

Wober, M. Explorations of the concept of self-esteem. *International Journal of Psychology*, vol. 6, no. 2, pp. 147–55, 1971.

Wood, J.B. Out of work and out of the figures. *New Society*, pp. 114–15, 20 April 1972.

Zawadski, B. and Lazarsfeld, P.* The psychological consequences of unemployment. *Journal of Social Psychology*, vol. 6, pp. 224–51, 1935.   **9, 20, 22, 23, 24, 111, 120**

# Subject Index